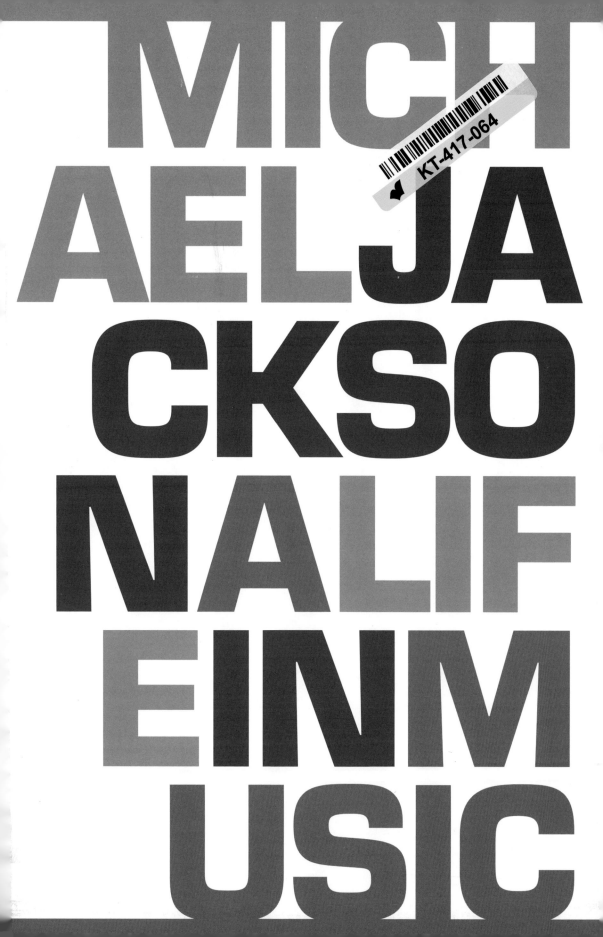

MICH
AELJA
CKSO
NALIF
EINM
USIC

Exclusive Distributors
Music Sales Limited, 14/15 Berners Street, London, W1T 3LJ.

Music Sales Corporation,
257 Park Avenue South, New York, NY 10010, USA.

Macmillan Distribution Services,
56 Parkwest Drive, Derrimut, Vic 3030, Australia.

Cover and book design by Fresh Lemon.
Front cover photography by Getty Images; back cover and text pages by LFI.

Every effort has been made to trace the copyright holders of the photographs
in this book but one or two were unreachable. We would be grateful if the
photographers concerned would contact us.

Printed by Caligraving Limited, UK.

A catalogue record for this book is available from the British Library.
Visit Omnibus Press on the web at www.omnibuspress.com

MICHAEL JACKSON
A LIFE IN MUSIC

GEOFF BROWN

OMNIBUS PRESS

LONDON / NEW YORK / PARIS / SYDNEY / COPENHAGEN / BERLIN / MADRID / TOKYO

1958
AUGUST 29

Michael Joseph Jackson is the seventh child born to Katherine and Joe Jackson in Gary, Indiana. Other Jackson siblings are: Maureen Reilette (Rebbie), 29 May, 1950; Sigmund Esco (Jackie), 4 May, 1951; Toriano Adaryl (Tito), 15 October, 1953; Jermaine La Juan, 11 December, 1954; Yvonne LaToya, 29 May, 1956; Marlon David, 12 March, 1957; Steven Randall (Randy), 29 October, 1961; Janet Damita, 16 May, 1966

1960

Father Joe begins coaching Jermaine, Tito and Jackie in his spare time and they are soon joined by Marlon and Michael. Joe later recruits drummer Johnny Jackson.

1969
OCTOBER

'I Want You Back'/'Who's Loving You', the Jackson 5's début single, is released on Motown Records and sells two million copies in six weeks. This is the group's first Gold record but, because Motown is not a member of the RIAA, it is not certified as such.

Diana Ross Presents The Jackson 5 enters both the Black and Pop album charts peaking at number 1, holding its position for nine and five weeks respectively. The LP spends a total of 32 weeks on the Pop charts.

1965

Joseph Jackson sends Motown founder, Berry Gordy, a tape of the Jackson 5. Three months later, it is returned with no offer.

1963
AUTUMN

Michael starts Kindergarten at Garnett Elementary School in Gary and, at the age of five, participates in a school pageant, singing an a cappella version of 'Climb Every Mountain' taken from the film *The Sound Of Music*. His emotional delivery brings his teacher and his mother to tears. This is Michael's first public performance. Shortly afterwards, Michael takes over from Jermaine as lead vocalist in the group.

1967

The Jackson 5 are seen by Gladys Knight at a show in Chicago. They subsequently perform at New York's Harlem Theatre where Michael gets to see James Brown.

1968
JANUARY

The Jackson 5 release the single 'Big Boy' on Steeltown Records, Gary. After an appearance on the David Frost TV show, The Jackson 5 audition for Berry Gordy, head of Motown Records, and are are subsequently signed to the label. The Jackson 5, father Joe and his assistant Jack Richardson are temporarily accommodated at the Hollywood Hills homes of Berry Gordy and Diana Ross.

1970
JANUARY

'I Want You Back'/'Who's Loving You' by the Jackson 5 enters the Top 50 singles chart in Britain, peaking at number 2, and remains on the charts for 13 weeks, selling over 250,000 copies. It hits number 1 on both the Pop and Black singles charts, holds its position for one and four weeks respectively and remains on the Pop charts for 19 weeks.

1970
APRIL

'ABC' hits number 1 on the Pop singles chart, replacing The Beatles' 'Let It Be', holding its position for two weeks and remaining on the charts for 13 weeks.

1970
SEPTEMBER

'I'll Be There'/'One More Chance' by the Jackson 5, released in August by Motown Records, enters the Black singles chart. It peaks at number 1 holding its position for six weeks and remaining on the charts for 13 weeks.

The Jackson 5 reach sales of 10 million worldwide for the singles 'I Want You Back,' 'ABC' and 'The Love You Save' during a nine-month period – a record unsurpassed in such a time period. The Jacksons move to their parents' first home in Encino, California.

1970
DECEMBER

The Jackson 5 embark on their first national tour playing shows in Boston, Cincinnati, Tennessee and New York City. There are incidents during these shows of teenage girls fainting, and trying to mount the stage. While on tour, the Jackson 5 are accompanied by a private tutor, Rose Fine.

1970
MAY

'The Love You Save'/'I Found That Girl' by the Jackson 5, released on May 13 by Motown Records, enters the Pop singles chart. It goes on to sell over two million copies.

The Jackson 5 play their first major concert at the Los Angeles Forum.

1971
APRIL

Michael appears on the cover of *Rolling Stone* magazine. Throughout the summer the Jackson 5 play their second major US tour, including a date in front of 80,000 fans at the Lake Michigan Summer Festival.

1972
JANUARY

'Got To Be There', Michael's first solo single, released.

1972
FEBRUARY

Got To Be There, Michael's first solo album, released on January 24 by Motown Records, enters the Black and Pop albums charts, peaking at numbers 3 and 14 respectively, and remains on the Pop charts for 23 weeks.

1974
JANUARY

The Jackson 5 perform in several African countries.

1972
AUGUST

Ben, Michael's second solo LP, is released, along with the eponymous single.

1972
NOVEMBER

The Jackson 5 arrive in the UK for their first British dates. While in Europe they also visit Amsterdam, Brussels, Frankfurt and Paris.

1973
JUNE/JULY

The Jackson 5 tour Australia.

1973
MARCH

'Ben' is nominated for an Oscar at the Academy Awards but doesn't win.

1973
APRIL/MAY

The Jackson 5 tour Japan.

1975
MAY

The Jackson 5, including Michael, announce they have signed with Epic Records, a subsidiary of Columbia, and will therefore leave Motown when their contract expires in 1976. Because Jermaine Jackson, who is married to Berry Gordy's daughter, remains with Motown, the group is renamed The Jacksons. Legal battles ensue but in the end the family stay with Epic.

1974
OCTOBER/ NOVEMBER

Far East tour by the Jackson 5.

1977
MAY

In the UK, the Jacksons play the Royal Command Performance as part of the Queen's Silver Jubilee celebrations.

1975
FEBRUARY

The Jackson 5 tour the UK

1976
JUNE

The Jacksons star in their own variety series on CBS TV.

1974
APRIL

The Jackson Family, including sisters Rebbie, La Toya and Janet, play the MGM Grand in Las Vegas. They return there twice before the end of the year.

1977
JULY

Michael rehearses for his role as the Scarecrow in Universal Pictures' remake of *The Wizard Of Oz, The Wiz,* which also stars Diana Ross as Dorothy. Filming begins in October when Michael meets the show's musical director, Quincy Jones, for the first time.

1978
DECEMBER

Destiny, the first Jacksons album on Epic, is released

1978

Michael meets Paul McCartney for the first time.

1979
AUGUST

Off The Wall, Michael's first solo LP on which he has full creative control, is released. Produced by Quincy Jones, it breaks music industry records by being the first album to include four Top Ten singles in the US. In the UK there are a record five hit singles, including 'Girlfriend', a duet with Paul McCartney.

1978
OCTOBER

The Wiz opens in Los Angeles.

1979
JANUARY

The Jacksons begin a world tour to promote their *Destiny* album, opening in Germany and moving on for several concerts in the UK.

1981
JULY

The Jacksons' Triumph tour opens in Memphis but some shows are cancelled after Michael collapses with exhaustion.

1980
OCTOBER

The Jacksons release their *Triumph* album.

1985
JANUARY

Michael and 44 other artists, including Bob Dylan and Bruce Springsteen, record 'We Are The World' co-written by Michael and Lionel Richie. This follows Bob Geldof's Band Aid initiative in the UK, which is designed to ease famine in Africa.

1985
AUGUST

Michael acquires ATV Music, which includes Northern Songs, The Beatles' publishing catalogue, from Australian millionaire Robert Holmes A'Court, for $47.5 million. The purchase does not please Paul McCartney.

1983
MAY

While singles from *Thriller*, including 'Billie Jean', 'Beat It' and the title track, are huge hits across the globe, Michael debuts his moonwalk dance during a TV show that celebrates Motown's 25th Anniversary.

Watched by 47,000,000 US viewers, it reinforces Michael's dominance of the music scene during a year when *Thriller* spent all 52 weeks of the year in the US Top Ten, including 37 at number one.

1987
AUGUST

Bad, Michael's third and final album produced by Quincy Jones, is released.

1982
DECEMBER

Michael's *Thriller*, which will go on to become the biggest-selling album of all time, is released.

1984
JULY

Michael is reunited with his brothers for the Victory tour, named after the Jacksons album released this month, opens in Kansas. The tour is dogged by poor organisation and some fans stay away because the price of tickets is too high. Nevertheless the tour continues through December.

1984
JANUARY

Michael wins an unprecedented eight awards at the Grammys in Los Angeles.

Michael's hair catches fire during the filming of a Pepsi commercial in New York.

1988
FEBRUARY/MARCH/APRIL

Michael starts his first ever solo tour of the US, opening in Kansas City. The tour continues through April.

1987
NOVEMBER

The Bad tour moves to Australia.

1988
SEPTEMBER/ OCTOBER

The Bad tour continues with more dates in the US.

1987
SEPTEMBER

Michael opens his solo Bad tour in Japan.

1988
MAY/JUNE/JULY

The Bad tour moves to Europe, opening in Rome.

1989
JANUARY

The Bad tour winds down with more shows in the US.

1988
JULY

Michael performs five sell-out concerts at London's Wembley Stadium, including one attended by Price Charles and Princess Diana.

1991
MARCH

Michael re-signs his contract with Sony Music, which had bought CBS in 1988. It is reported to be the biggest music deal in history.

Michael is seen dining out with Madonna in Los Angeles.

1993
JANUARY

Michael performs at the Super Bowl Half Time Show at the Rose Bowl Stadium, Pasadena. It is watched by 100,000 in the stadium and 133 million on TV.

1989
DECEMBER

Michael is on the cover of *Vanity Fair* magazine, with a picture taken by Annie Leibovitz.

1992
FEBRUARY

Michael visits West Africa.

1992
JULY/AUGUST/SEPTEMBER

Michael's European tour again includes five concerts at Wembley Stadium

1991
NOVEMBER

Michael's single 'Black Or White', featuring Guns N' Roses guitarist Slash, is released.

Michael's *Dangerous* album is released.

1992
DECEMBER

Japanese tour.

1995
JUNE
Michael's *HIStory* album is released throughout the world.

1993
AUGUST/ SEPTEMBER
Far East tour, followed by shows in Moscow and Tel Aviv.

1994
SEPTEMBER
Child molestation charges relating to Jordan Chandler are dropped.

1993
AUGUST
The LA Police Department investigates allegations of abuse made by 13-year-old Jordan Chandler.

1993
DECEMBER
Michael makes a statement denying the child abuse allegations.

1996
JANUARY
It is reported that Michael has separated from Lisa Marie Presley.

1993
OCTOBER/ NOVEMBER
Michael tours South America and Mexico. Further dates on the Dangerous tour are cancelled due to Michael's addiction to pain-killing drugs.

1994
MAY
Michael marries Elvis Presley's daughter, Lisa Marie, in the Dominican Republic. News of the marriage is not released until July.

1996
DECEMBER
The HIStory tour visits Japan and other Far Eastern countries.

1996
JULY
Michael attends a private birthday party for Nelson Mandela in South Africa.

1997
JANUARY
Michael plays two concerts in Hawaii, his first US dates since 1989.

1996
FEBRUARY
Michael's appearance at the Brits in London is disrupted when Pulp singer Jarvis Cocker runs on stage while Michael sings 'Earth Song'.

1997
FEBRUARY
Debbie Rowe gives birth to Michael's son Prince Michael in Los Angeles.

1997
MAY/JUNE/JULY/AUGUST
The second leg of the HIStory tour, which opens in Germany, crosses Europe, and includes three concerts at London's Wembley Stadium.

1996
SEPTEMBER
Michael attracts 120,000 fans to a concert in Warsaw, Poland.

1996
NOVEMBER
It is announced that Michael has married 37-year-old nurse Debbie Rowe during a ceremony in Australia where he is playing concerts.

1998
APRIL

Michael's wife Debbie Rowe gives birth to a baby girl, Paris Michael Katherine Jackson.

2002
JULY

Michael speaks out against the American music industry's treatment of black artists, and claims that Sony have not sufficiently promoted *Invincible*.

1999
OCTOBER

Michael and Debbie Rowe end their marriage.

2001
SEPTEMBER

Michael performs at two tribute concerts for him at New York's Madison Square Garden.

2000
NOVEMBER

Michael talks about his forthcoming album, on which he will collaborate with several different producers.

2001
OCTOBER

Michael takes part in a marathon concert in Washington, organised to benefit the victims of the 9/11 World Trade Centre atrocity.

1999
APRIL

In London, Michael attends a football match at Craven Cottage, home of Fulham FC. The club is owned by Harrods boss Mohammed Al Fayed, whose son Dodi died in the Paris crash in 1997 that killed Diana, Princess of Wales.

2001
NOVEMBER

Michael's album *Invincible* is released.

2003
FEBRUARY

The controversial documentary *Living With Michael Jackson* is aired on TV. Later Michael issues a statement claiming he was "unfairly treated".

2005
JANUARY/FEBRUARY/ MARCH/APRIL/MAY

Michael's trial for child abuse continues.

2003
NOVEMBER

More child abuse allegations lead LA police to search Michael's Neverland Valley Ranch in Santa Barbara. Michael is subsequently arrested and charged.

2004
MAY

A tentative date is set for Michael's child abuse trial but it is further delayed until 2005.

2003
JUNE

Michael is back in Gary, Indiana, to receive the keys of the city and revisit his childhood home.

2004
DECEMBER

Armed with a new search warrant, police raid Michael's Neverland Ranch for a second time.

2002
NOVEMBER

In Germany, Michael holds his new baby Prince Michael II over the railings high up in his hotel suite. He later apologises for his actions.

2005
SEPTEMBER

Michael flies to the Middle East, where he stays as a guest of Bahrain's Southern Governor Sheikh Abdullah bin Hamad Al Khalifa.

2009
JUNE 25

Michael dies from a heart attack at a rented home in Los Angeles.

2006

For most of the year, Michael stays in Bahrain, making periodic visits to London, Ireland, Paris and Hamburg.

2005
JUNE

Michael is found not guilty of the abuse charges.

2007

Michael takes up residence in Las Vegas, but maintains a low profile for much of the year amid continuing reports about problems with his financial affairs.

2008

Celebrating the 25th anniversary of *Thriller, Thriller 25* is released, containing remixes and a previously unreleased song.

To celebrate Jackson's 50th birthday in August, Sony BMG releases a compilation album.

2009
MARCH

In London, Michael announces that he will perform 50 shows at the O2 Arena from July 13, 2009, to March 6, 2010.

Michael Jackson was breaking records as a big-selling pop star before he was a teenager and went on to set standards for commercial success by selling upwards of 50 million copies of one piece of work, *Thriller.* His other solo albums recorded as an adult have sold in the region of another 50 million and he sold millions of singles as a child star fronting The Jackson 5. He became one of the richest individuals in the world.

INTRODU

He could have anything he wanted and do anything he wanted. He could be anything he wanted except private, a child again or immortal and some of those things are probably what he most wanted. He was not a poor little rich boy who inherited wealth. His fortune was generated by his talent. As a child he had no choice or control over how this talent was directed but he learned his crafts – singing, dancing, recording, writing – with a speed and thoroughness that impressed his elders.

The price exacted for these riches was well documented in a series of biographies, his personal memoir (he was too young to have written a definitive autobiography) and the biographies and autobiographies of other members of his family. You might know of large families, ruled by fear of the father, who have evolved to be every bit as dysfunctional as the Jacksons without the professional pressures – or the opportunities for counselling money can buy. Of course, wealth could not forever shore up a collapsing family structure. Look at the Windsors. It is ludicrous to expect that Michael Jackson (b 29 August, 1958) should have grown up "ordinary". His was not an ordinary childhood. Jackie (b Sigmund Esco Jackson, 4 May, 1951), Tito (b Toriano Adaryll Jackson, 15 October, 1953) and Jermaine (b Jermaine La Jaune Jackson, 11 December, 1954), his three elder brothers, formed a trio in 1961.

CTION

Michael joined a few years later (with Marlon David Jackson, b 12 March, 1957), his singing and dancing thrusting him to the fore. He'd been fronting the group for six years when the commercial ball started rolling in 1969. He was 11, something of a veteran and fast becoming the family's meal ticket. He, not the father, was their breadwinner. And for a short while he was central to Motown's financial stability.

Remarkably, he was one of the few child stars who was a bigger star as an adult. Although Motown had parlayed a "child genius" Little Stevie Wonder into a mature star, the burn-out rate among pop music child stars is roughly equal to that of movie child stars. In 1956, Frankie Lymon & The Teenagers had four R&B hits in the US, two of which were Top 20 pop hits there, and 'Why Do Fools Fall In Love?', which Lymon

had written at the age of 13, got to No 1 in the UK, the first of three British hits. Addicted to heroin for much of the Sixties, he died of an overdose in 1968, a year before The Jackson 5 burst onto the scene. By these tokens, Michael's career should have ended in the Seventies.

The 5's success in targeting a new, young audience spawned a rash of imitations, notably The Osmonds (a bizarre Battle of the Sects subtext here: Jehovah's Witnesses versus The Mormons!). Since then, the teen and pre-teen market has never been without succour – New Edition, New Kids On The Block, Take That, East 17, Boyzone, rap acts like Kriss Kross, vocal groups who, as did the J5, base their acts on the vocal legacy of Sixties soul (Boyz II Men, Jodeci and so on) in Nineties clothes and dances.

According to some books, his father, a manipulator by fear, told Jackson he was not as good as he thought. Motown told him he was fabulous but had much to learn. When he thought he'd learned much and wanted some control, they told him he wasn't as good as he thought. The press wrote that he was great, then not as good as he thought. Then he was fantastic, then weird, mad and much worse. He formed few lasting relationships with people of his own age outside his family because of the cocoon woven around him by family and record company, by his own shyness (another result of a cloistered upbringing), and by his dissatisfaction with his appearance, which was not helped by virulent teenage acne, teasing brothers and a taunting father.

The rest you will have read about in the newspapers.

PART I
THE
JACKSON 5

In the beginning was The Corporation. And The Corporation was Mighty. And The Corporation saw The Jackson 5 home video and saw that it was good. For Bobby Taylor, leader of The Vancouvers, a toiler in soul's vineyard, hath seen The Jackson 5 many times and had spoken unto Gladys Knight of their great talent.
And Gladys Knight hath seen them at the Regal Theater, Chicago in 1967 and sent word to her Lord and Master at The Corporation, whose name shall be honoured for it is (all rise) Berry Gordy (all sit). And Berry Gordy called a Great Gathering of acolytes to his Mansion and they were much excited. For there had been consternation in The Corporation that it was losing its powers and that its flock was wandering elsewhere, yea, even unto the false gods of Psychedelic Rock, unto emerging sects who worshipped Funk, and unto the politicised scribes who spake the words Black Power.

Certainly, in the way it came to be told, there was something Biblical rather than merely providential about the "discovery" of The Jackson 5, a group of teens and pre-teenagers rigorously tutored by their father, Joe Jackson, in the over-spilling family home at Gary, Indiana. They had recorded a couple of undistinguished singles for Steeltown,

Whitfield's Temptations' productions. What the signing *did* achieve was to re-energize the company and reaffirm its slogan, The Sound Of Young America, by shooting it back to the top of the singles charts four times in 11 months as The Jackson 5 became the first new group to hit No 1 with its first four singles.

"It was Tito who decided we should form a group and we did and we practised a lot and then we started entering talent shows and we won every one we entered."

a local label in Michigan, before word-of-mouth, a home video and an audition at Berry's pad got them a deal with Tamla Motown records, which was in the process of moving to Los Angeles – Gordy wanted to break into movies big time and was not fascinated by Detroit's inner-city problems.

The label was also in the process of re-grouping after the loss of its main hit-writing team – Brian Holland, Lamont Dozier, Eddie Holland – and a sudden sea change in the music market that was affecting sales of singles, traditionally the main aim of "black" music in general (jazz was the exception) and Motown in particular. Previously, African-American music had not been attuned to album sales, but it was now the growth area in the "white" music market, the market that had turned Berry's labels – Tamla, Gordy and Motown – from an exciting local operation into a national phenomenon, one of the largest black-owned companies in the United States and a beacon of pride and achievement to a people.

The signing of The Jackson 5 did not give Motown sudden penetration into the albums market – that came within a couple of years through the extraordinary fertile period of recording by Marvin Gaye ('What's Going On', 'Let's Get It On') and Stevie Wonder ('Music Of My Mind', 'Talking Book', 'Innervisions', 'Fulfillingness' First Finale') and Norman

The 5 had been performing on stage since 1965, were winning high-profile talent contests two years later and in 1967 played at the Apollo Theater in Harlem, New York. They were not entirely unknown outside a small area of Michigan when Motown signed them and travelled as far east and south as Philadelphia, Kansas City and St Louis to support big name acts but made little noise, even locally, with the ballad 'Big Boy' backed with 'You've Changed' (1968) on Steeltown. (To collectors, an original copy is now worth a cool grand.) A second Steeltown single, the teenybop precursor 'You Don't Have To Be Over 21 To Fall In Love' with a 'Jam Session' flip, recorded in 1968, was eventually released in 1971 in a futile attempt to cash in on their subsequent breakthrough. Another Steeltown single, by The Ripples Featuring Michael (aka The Ripple & The Waves) and titled 'Let Me Carry Your Schoolbooks'/'I Never Had A Girl', was also released in 1971, though the label denied it was by The Jackson 5. But by the end of 1968 they'd been signed by Motown and relocated to Los Angeles, living as guests in the not unpalatial homes of Gordy and his label's hot property Diana Ross. (The Steeltown sides are available as 'The Jackson 5 Featuring Michael Jackson: Historic Early Recordings' on Charly Groove CPCD 8122. There is also a more extensive and expensive Japanese import titled 'Big Boy'.)

Once the deal with The Jackson 5 had been struck, Motown took over the grooming of the act from daddy Joe. The seasoned dance and deportment professionals who had taught the established breadwinners – The Supremes, The Temptations, The Miracles, The Four Tops – were now only fine-tuning, occasionally devising new steps but mostly trying to keep each act fresh and functioning. With The Jackson 5 they had a whole new pasture to cultivate and a younger Motown staffer, Suzanne de Passe, who was more in tune with the group's potential audience, as well as the group itself, was charged with getting the young boys up to Motown speed. Of course, age was not the only difference. Motown was essentially built on acts that sang and danced. The Jackson 5, like a growing number of popular African-American acts, played their own instruments too. There was a grand amount of practice to be done here too.

As a songwriter, Berry Gordy knew the importance of good material to any act – penning hits for Jackie Wilson ('Reet Petite', 'To Be Loved', 'Lonely Teardrops', 'That's Why (I Love You So)', 'I'll Be Satisfied', all US Pop Top 20 hits) taught him that. He nurtured songwriters, like Holland-Dozier-Holland and Smokey Robinson, with as much care and criticism as he lavished on performers. A writing and production grouping that he had put together – and was part of – was The Corporation, a faceless name, like The Clan, an earlier Motown agglomeration that had written for Diana Ross & The Supremes, among others. In addition to Gordy, The Corporation was Freddie Perren, Alphonso "Fonce" Mizell and Deke Richards with assists from Taylor and Hal Davis. Using an idea of Gordy's they wrote 'I Want You Back', the Jacksons' first single released in October, 1969. By the end of January, 1970 it was No 1 in the US and had sold two million copies, while in the UK pop charts it was just breaking into the charts *en route* to a high of No 2.

In true, tried and tested Motown tradition, the group's first album, whacked out to cash in on their erupting popularity, had all the hallmarks of a hastily slapped together piece of work. The credits, however, suggested otherwise. The producers were Bobby Taylor, a thank you for "discovering" them, and The Corporation. The arrangers: The Corp, again, plus David Van De Pitte, Paul Riser and David Blumberg. There was a wide spread of material from standards and Walt Disney to Motown classics and new pop-funk. Although there are unquestionably a couple of failures among the dozen tracks, the record succeeds because it focuses on, and captures, the young group's zest and exuberance, Michael's in particular.

In an inspired, calculating notion, the group was officially launched on *The Hollywood Palace Special*, an ABC-TV show hosted by Diana Ross & The Supremes, but had created an extremely favourable impression with appearances on *The Ed Sullivan*, *Johnny Carson* and *Soul Train* US TV shows, at around the time the group's début album was released. If you were to nominate three TV shows to give you blanket coverage of the 1969 American singles-buying market, it was those three.

Clockwise: Tito, Jackie, Jermaine, Marlon & Michael

DIANA ROSS PRESENTS THE JACKSON 5

Tamla Motown STML 11142
UK release March, 1970
UK CD No: ZD 72483 with ABC album

ZIP-A-DEE DOO-DAH

It's hard to imagine a better song with which to open a (very) young group's first album. A hummable tune with a very simple, direct and happy-go-lucky lyric, its atmosphere set the agenda for the first period of the group's career. Popularised in Walt Disney's *The Song Of The South* (1946) and a hit for Bob B Soxx & The Blue Jeans under the auspices of Phil Spector in 1962, 'Zip-A-Dee Doo-Dah' was reworked in a funkier vein. Michael's exuberant "Yeah, Yeah" shouts descended the scale into Motown's churning interpretation of funk – not as convincing as Norman Whitfield's visions in funk would be later down the line, but that is hardly the point. Gordy said that his model for The Jackson 5's early records was Frankie Lymon & The Teenagers and, in this respect, youthful exuberance in a modern setting fits the role.

NOBODY

A good Corporation song. Like several of the tracks on each Jackson 5 album, it relies on the interplay between the voices of Michael and Jermaine. The youthful energy with which they blast through the lyrics ("Money in the bank don't mean a thing" – it's odd, isn't it, that only well-off people write that kind of stuff?) and

the fullness of the arrangement build a sustaining second track. Bass guitar batters sixteenths as the song drives hard to the fade.

I WANT YOU BACK

Despite the Steeltown single, which crept out to general disinterest, this is considered to be the 5's début and on a North American and certainly international basis, that's fair. As such, the Motown début single announced the group forcefully and confidently. Certainly the opening to 'I Want You Back' exploded out of the radio speakers with extraordinary vitality – a swoop down the piano keyboard introduces Morse-code guitar chording as bass guitar and piano in unison hammer out an emphatic riff. This was music that rushed over, grabbed you by the arm. C'mere, c'mere! Hear this! The broken arrangement, with uptempo, modern doo-wop sections *à la* Sly & The Family Stone, show the arrangers fully aware of everything that was happening out there, just as they're in tune with the inner workings of the group.

The playing, the group's vocals or the brief interjection of another brother, all set up

Michael's high-soaring lead. For example, to close out the group's doo-wop section the nine-year-old's improbably impassioned "All I want, All I need/All I want, All I neeeeed!" leads back into the main body of the song in a distant echo of the tumbling descent of piano keys that kick-started the single. When trading "Babys!" with Jermaine it is clear which voice most wants his "Baby!" in spite of the discrepancy in age (Jermaine was 14, quite the old geezer). It was Michael's ability to mimic, absorb the influence and then quickly reinterpret as something of his own that separated him from his brothers as a talent. In his autobiography, *Moonwalk*, Jackson said that they spent more time recording this one track than the rest of the album put together. It was written by The Corporation from a kernel of melody floating in Gordy's brain, according to the label-owner's autobiography, *To Be Loved*. In fact, it had been written as 'I Want To Be Free' for Gladys Knight & The Pips. It sold six million.

CAN YOU REMEMBER
Written by master arranger and producer Thom Bell with The Delfonics' William Hart, the song, not surprisingly, is in the sweet Philly soul style and one of the least convincing tracks on the album.

STANDING IN THE SHADOWS OF LOVE
Holland-Dozier-Holland had not long jumped ship and had been doing legal battle with Gordy's company for alleged mis-accounting of royalties and other contract infractions. It had been settled, not amicably, out of court. Here, Gordy uses one of the hits they'd written for The Four Tops. Dilemma: The song has been emphatically stamped for all time by Levi Stubbs' classic performance. How can a nine-year-old perform it with conviction? Answer: Deconstruct. The Four Tops version opens with Stubbs' marvellously assertive voice. For The Jackson 5, bongos and guitar ease the song open at a slightly, but perceptibly, slower pace; it's hard to believe Norman Whitfield didn't devise this treatment.

Like the Tops, a verse is sung first. Then, like Stubbs, Michael sings "I wanna *run...*" and squeezes as much emotion out of it as we've a right to expect from a pre-teen. For the 5, the instrumental decoration of the track is more complex and their vocals are pulled back into the mix whereas Stubbs' maturer voice boomed out.

YOU'VE CHANGED
With new label-mates Smokey Robinson & The Miracles as the clear blueprint, the song's story – a young, ugly duckling of a girl grows into a beautiful swan – is perfect for the market. The lyric connects with an older audience too – "girl," Michael sings, "when I look at you, all the love come runnin' through". There's some good call-and-response between the group and Michael. In all, a very "up" sound.

MY CHERIE AMOUR
Sung by Jermaine, a straight take on Stevie Wonder's hit.

WHO'S LOVIN' YOU
A song written for himself and The Miracles by Smokey Robinson and given a fairly faithful reading here by Michael in an astonishingly mature performance,

where the mimic's artifice crosses over into a new territory and becomes interpretation. Only very occasionally is it obvious that the pipes voicing these emotions belong not to a man singing falsetto but to a child.

Of course, some of that may have to do with familiarity with Smokey's exquisite original in his inimitable, sky-high tenor. But, even so, it's a sound performance. The track was the B-side to 'I Want You Back'.

CHAINED

Written by Frank Wilson and a Top 10 R&B hit for Marvin Gaye in 1968, it's another of the least interesting or successful performances on the album. Gaye did it so well, of course, because he felt "chained" to his wife, Anna Gordy, and to a recording style he did not enjoy. Despite the shackles of their suffocating family environment, The Jackson 5 were on the crest of a wave and, at this time, "chained" was the last thing they felt.

(I KNOW) I'M LOSING YOU

One of Norman Whitfield's classic early productions on The Temptations, The Jackson 5 do little with it. Michael does not sing lead.

STAND

If anything, their version of the Sly & The Family Stone hit sounds over-arranged. At this point The Corporation production team is more comfortable with covers of Motown hits from the mid-Sixties than with the new funk.

BORN TO LOVE YOU

Michael and Jermaine share vocal duties more evenly on a song co-written by Motown staffers Joe Hunter and William Mickey Stevenson. Pleasant, but not a highlight.

ABC

Tamla Motown STML 11156
UK release August, 1970
Motown CD 3746351522
and ZD 72483, with Diana Ross
Presents Jacksons 5

The Corporation wasted little time in hammering home the message. The group was back on TV promoting the March, 1970 release of their second single, 'ABC', before the first album came out, while 'I Want You Back', the single, was still in the charts. Tracks recorded while taping the Diana Ross show were released in March, 1970 on *Motown At The Hollywood Palace,* a various artists compilation. The group's second album, same title as the second single, came out in the US in June, 1970, six months after the first album. In the UK it came out two months later. In the US it reached No 4, in the UK, No 22. There were twice as many songs by The Corporation among the 12 tracks, the remainder again being predominantly a mixture of soul staples from, and outside, the company. Hal Davis co-produced with The Corporation. After the *Diana Ross Presents* album sleeve, which grouped the 5 in a line of ascending height with Michael at the front and looking back past him to Jackie at the back, this album had them pictured leaning against outsize letters of the title. It has the effect of making Michael and Marlon seem tiny compared to Jackie, Tito and Jermaine.

THE LOVE YOU SAVE
The third single and consecutive No 1 hit and a very merry sound, adding a profoundly pop energy to the vocal mix of Michael and the group. The extremely youthful quality of the leader's voice is made best use of by constant reference to the school playground and nursery rhyme in a melody that echoes that of the album's title track. Again, the interplay between Michael and Jermaine gives the song an extra edge.

 **2-4-6-8**
Never afraid to milk an idea bone dry, Motown writers Pam Sawyer and Leon Ware constructed a measured, mid-tempo guitar-drums track for another love song based on playground rhymes as in "2-4-6-8, who do you appreciate".

(COME ROUND HERE) I'M THE ONE YOU NEED
Precocious is the best, indeed only description of Michael's spirited version of

"The thing I remember most from those days – and the reason we are here today as entertainers – was rehearsing for seven hours every day. Straight after school, perfecting ourselves with our father teaching us. He taught me exactly how to hold a mike and make gestures to the crowd and how to handle an audience... he was the best teacher we could have had."

 ONE MORE CHANCE
A mid-tempo ballad and The Corporation's first experiment. Filler, really, but Michael exudes confidence.

 ABC
And what, indeed, could be easier than learning ABC? With the working title of '1-2-3', Deke Richards' original idea for the follow-up to 'I Want You Back', conceived at the behest of Gordy, quite blatantly leaned almost solely on simple images of children's playground games. But the *joie de vivre* with which the group performs the pure pop is utterly infectious and the group's vocals now sound as confident as Michael's. In his autobiography, *Moonwalk*, he cited it as one of his three favourite Jackson 5 tracks. The others were 'Never Can Say Goodbye' and 'I'll Be There'.

the 1966 Miracles' hit written by Holland-Dozier-Holland. Although lacking some of Smokey's wistful lilt, he nonetheless brings an uncanny conviction of his own to the lyric.

DON'T KNOW WHY I LOVE YOU
A straight reading of the song that formed a double-sided hit with 'My Cherie Amour' for Stevie Wonder in 1969. Michael is an impressive mimic of Wonder's vocal patterns but, as yet, can't quite match the passion.

NEVER HAD A DREAM COME TRUE
Another minor Stevie Wonder hit, this time from 1970. Motown's success at breaking Wonder as a teen act was playing heavily on the minds of The Corporation. This version totally misses the song's potential for wistful reading.

 TRUE LOVE CAN BE BEAUTIFUL
Credited to Bobby Taylor and J Jackson, that's J as in daddy Joe, this is Motown filler – with all the signatures of arrangement, both vocal and instrumental, a decent hook but no major melody.

 LA LA (MEANS I LOVE YOU)
The album's Philly groove is another Thom Bell and William Hart collaboration, which was the 1968 breakthrough hit for Hart's group The Delfonics. For once, the song seems too adult for the J5, whose youthful piping grates harshly against the sophisticated melody and tender emotions the song attempts to express.

 I'LL BET YOU
A 1969 hit for Funkadelic. In The Jackson 5's hands the George Clinton song sounds as much like an attempt to recreate a Norman Whitfield-styled psychedelic funk production for The Temptations as a wild Funkadelic

extemporisation. Problem with the version is that the 5 simply didn't have the vocal spread to match Funkadelic's or, indeed, the Temps' vocal palette.

I FOUND THAT GIRL
The B-side of 'The Love You Save', this Corporation song provided Jermaine with his best lead opportunity in that breakthrough year. The image of a young, mid-teen singer telling his mom about finding the perfect girl sent palpitations through the hearts of young America. Me! Me! the girls all shouted.

THE YOUNG FOLKS
"You better make way for the young folk," warns Michael, in The Jackson 5's first excursion into "protest". And they are not demanding later bed-time and more pocket money, they mean "business". The B-side of 'ABC'.

CHRISTMAS ALBUM

UK Tamla Motown STML 11168
released December, 1970.
CD Spectrum 550 141-2

What to say about a seasonal cash-in other than that, in the circumstances, the kids sing the mixture of carols and Christmas

THE THIRD ALBUM

Tamla Motown STML11174
UK release February, 1971
CD 530 160-2

By September, 1970, when 'Third' was released in the US, The Jackson 5's three chirpy and uptempo singles – 'I Want You

"He [his father] can be very hard... sometimes. You don't wanna be getting him mad. He's strict but we never object. That's how he wants it so we go along. He shows us the value of work and hard effort."

standards with as much innocence as possible. But the Phil Spector Christmas album, it ain't. The tracks are – 'Have Yourself A Merry Little Christmas', 'Santa Claus Is Coming To Town', 'The Christmas Song', 'Up On The Housetop', 'Frosty The Snowman', 'The Little Drummer Boy', 'Rudolph The Red-Nosed Reindeer', 'Christmas Won't Be The Same This Year', 'Give Love On Christmas Day', 'Someday At Christmas', 'I Saw Mommy Kissing Santa Claus'. ('Santa Claus Is Coming To Town' backed with 'Christmas Won't Be The Same This Year' was the 1970 single.)

Back', 'ABC', 'The Love You Save' – had sold 10 million copies in nine months. The more intimate group portrait on the cover of the new album – the camera focuses in tight on their faces, which are lit from each side and behind, the shadows creating a moodier image – shows a fast-growing group. Their Afros have grown out slightly too. Michael, by now, has established his reputation among the Motown staff as a dedicated and very hard worker, keen to learn everything about the recording studio. There is less clutter about the sound of the record and a greater willingness to experiment with, for example, harpsichord ('I'll Be There') and flute ('Ready Or Not').

I'LL BE THERE

The fourth single was a ballad brought to Gordy by Willie Hutch and co-producer Hal Davis. Another writer, Bob West, had also worked on it. At the time, recording a slow song seemed a gamble, but it's one of the most-heard Jackson 5 singles from the early days because its melody and message of constancy transcend considerations of age. A goose-pimpler of a tune, Michael sings his sections at the top of his range with increasing freedom and expression; Jermaine's counterpoint is well-judged. That said, it is hard to imagine any established Motown act failing with the song.

It was the first single not credited to The Corporation but it still went to No 1 in the US and became Motown's third biggest seller of all time after Marvin Gaye's 'I Heard It Through The Grapevine' and 'Endless Love', the Diana Ross and Lionel Richie ballad. Hal Davis' oft-repeated story concerning Gordy's perfectionism, attention to detail and unwillingness to let a song go has the label owner ringing Davis in the wee small hours saying he'd just heard the song on the radio and it sounded as though Michael was being asked to sing too high. He thought they should re-cut. Was the record not selling, a concerned Davis asked? A pause. Gordy laughed. Only over two million in three days. The single stayed as it was.

READY OR NOT HERE I COME (CAN'T HIDE FROM LOVE)

The affair between The Jackson 5 and Thom Bell/William Hart songs continued with this respectable version of The Delfonics' 1968 hit.

OH HOW HAPPY

The 1966 Shades Of Blue hit provides another vehicle for Jermaine, which he could manage rather better than...

BRIDGE OVER TROUBLED WATER

The first big misjudgement. The young Jermaine's lead doesn't cope at all well with the drama of the melody and sweep of the arrangement of Simon & Garfunkel's grandstander. Here, it is turned into a heavy plod. The fade can't come soon enough.

CAN I SEE YOU IN THE MORNING

An interesting, if flawed, experiment in creating a pseudo-psychedelic mid-tempo ballad in the manner of the late-Sixties Beatles or Stones. The flaw occurs in the lyric. A younger man tries to persuade his older lover to let him see her in the morning "like I seen you late at night". "Come and hold me, make me feel all right," sings Michael, in just about the only early track on which the age of the singer actually seems inappropriate.

GOIN' BACK TO INDIANA

Straight-ahead, unpretentious rock 'n' roll 12-bar written by The Corporation and sung by Michael with huge gusto. "OK Tito, you got it," he yells to the

guitar-playing brother whose lack of fan mail clearly called for name-check. Despite the rootin' tootin' rah-rah for Indiana chant towards the end, they never went back to Gary, Indiana, all that often but did so in January, 1971, a trip captured by a TV special sharing the track's title.

HOW FUNKY IS YOUR CHICKEN

In an inter-group dance battle, the 5 get down in the funky playing and arrangement format of The Family Stone. True to Motown heritage, the track sounds as much like a Norman Whitfield production of The Temptations as it does a slice of Sly. The vocal is sung as first and second tenor plus falsetto. In the dance contest, there will have been only one winner.

MAMA'S PEARL
Back with The Corporation's uptempo hits, their fifth single was just a shade *too* obviously off the post-'I Want You Back' production line. As usual, there's lively interplay between Michael and Jermaine. It reached No 2 on the US pop

charts. Perhaps it would have fared better under its early working title, 'Who's Been Making Whoopee With My Girlfriend'.

REACH IN
Rather like being button-holed on one's doorstep by a couple of Americans wearing raincoats in August, this was the first song to give an indication of the devout side of the Jackson family. "Reach in," sings Michael, "find that tree of wisdom" and discover the purpose of your life.

THE LOVE I SAW IN YOU WAS JUST A MIRAGE

As noted previously, Smokey Robinson's high tenor sketched the perfect blueprint for any Jackson 5 vocal arrangement. 'Mirage', a very fine Smokey song, was the 1967 single on which The Miracles became Smokey Robinson &… It is impossible for a decent singer to find nothing in the song.

DARLING DEAR
Final filler track, there to pad out the album to 11 tracks.

MAYBE TOMORROW

Tamla Motown STML 11188
UK release October, 1971
CD No530 161-2.

That this was their fifth album in less than a year-and-a-half is ample evidence of the young act's heavy recording schedule. Occasional live performances and frequent guest appearances on TV shows, which replaced the grind of one-nighters in importance for promotion of the group, and the need to get some "proper" education make the early part of their career seem more like a race to get established than anything else. In fact, this would be the last time the owner of the label would get behind a recording project to such an extent, hence the energy, output and excitement.

The album was produced and arranged mostly by The Corporation with additional arrangements by Gene Page and James Carmichael, with five production credits for Hal Davis. The Corporation's writing for The Jackson 5 does not seem to have moved on much at all, and a couple of their songs are awful, yet Davis seems aware of the ageing process. Everyone was – the US launch of Michael's solo career came in October, 1971.

MAYBE TOMORROW
Is Michael's voice changing? There is more depth and resonance in the lower notes and less room at the top of his register, though he can still yell up there with the best. This encouraged The Corporation to be more adventurous when arranging what would become the second single off the album. Previously, they'd used several obvious models – The Miracles, The Temptations with Norman Whitfield, The Four Tops. Here, they go for the latter with a wholeheartedness missing from earlier Tops-based arrangements. The reflective ballad, written by The Corporation, builds from a rather unimpressive opening to a grand finale of swooping strings, thwacked snare drum and exultant vocals. The US market was not impressed, as after six singles with a lowest position of No 2, 'Tomorrow' peaked at No 20.

SHE'S GOOD
A pleasant vocal by Jermaine on one of The Corporation's less enthralling songs. It was the B-side of 'Never Can Say Goodbye', the album's first single.

NEVER CAN SAY GOODBYE
Probably recorded earlier in the sessions because Michael's voice still has a piping, reaching quality to it, 'Never Can Say Goodbye' was produced by Hal Davis, written by Clifton Davis and was the first single, later to be covered at length and in a somewhat earthier manner by Isaac Hayes. In the US a No 2 hit, it was one of Michael's three favourite Jackson 5 tracks.

THE WALL
Another Hal Davis production, written by Jerry Marcellino, Mel Larson and Pam Sawyer. The soul-clapping on the eighths gives each chorus a considerable lift. The central lyric image is "tearing down the walls between us". Larson and Marcellino would become frequent writer/producers for the brothers when the relationship between label and group was less cordial.

PETALS
Incredibly trite song by The Corporation containing many of your favourite Jackson 5 clichés squeezed into one package of ersatz teen pop-soul.

16 CANDLES

Inferior reworking at a faster pace of The Crests' 1959 doo-wop hit, Jermaine leads the celebrations of a 16-year-old's birthday. A Hal Davis production.

(WE'VE GOT) BLUE SKIES

Sung with a clear, innocent purity by Michael, this is nonetheless a messy, ill-advised and rather annoying track.

MY LITTLE BABY

Further indication that The Corporation, much older gentlemen than the group, had run out of ideas and were rehashing with energy but no inspiration ideas left over from their first brainstorming sessions on the project. Cute chorus, though, and not as bad as 'Petals'.

IT'S GREAT TO BE HERE

More warmed-over Corporation clichés. Even the previously irrepressible Michael seems to have difficulty getting believably excited about the song.

HONEY CHILE

Michael's introduction is hilarious, attempting a southern accent – "it was thair on my granma's fahm whair tha grapes grew hah on the vahne" – which would surely have brought him a charge of bringing African-Americans into disrepute at the local chapter of the NAACP were he an adult. The song, written by Richard Morris and Sylvia Moy, was a hit for Martha & The Vandellas, in a somewhat more cohesive and vigorous version, in 1967.

I WILL FIND A WAY

Jermaine's final contribution to the album. As ever, he does his level and willing best with an utterly predictable arrangement of dull material.

GOIN' BACK TO INDIANA

US Motown 742
released September, 1971

Ostensibly the soundtrack album to the ABC TV special that shared that name. Not released in the UK until the Pickwick label put it out in 1974 as *Stand!* As well as playing their hits, the 5 acted in comedy sketches, which featured guest appearances by Bill Cosby and The Smothers Brothers and were seen during a triumphal return to rootsville, Gary, Indiana. Tracks were: 'I Want You Back', 'Maybe Tomorrow', 'The Day Basketball Was Saved', 'Stand', 'I Want To Take You Higher', 'Feelin' Alright', 'Walk On By'/'The Love You Save', 'Goin' Back To Indiana'.

GREATEST HITS

UK Tamla Motown STML 11212,
released August, 1972
CD WD 72087

The essential Jackson 5 album with a mixture of group and very early Michael Jackson chartbusters, the better B-sides plus two singles that had not yet appeared on albums. Tracks were: Jackson 5 – 'I Want You Back', 'ABC', 'Never Can Say Goodbye', 'I'll Be There', 'Maybe Tomorrow', 'The Love You Save', 'Who's Lovin' You', 'Mama's Pearl', 'Goin' Back To Indiana', 'I Found That Girl'; Michael Jackson – 'Got To Be There', 'Rockin' Robin' (see separate section on Michael Jackson solo at Motown). New tracks:–

 LITTLE BITTY PRETTY ONE
First recorded by Bobby Day, a No 5 hit for Thurston Harris in 1957, and a No 13 hit for the group in May, 1972, 'Little Bitty Pretty One' is a chirpy, optimistic invitation from a young man to the cuddlesome one of his desire. Jackie, Jermaine and Michael share lead vocal duties.

LOOKIN' THROUGH THE WINDOWS

UK Tamla Motown STML 11214
released October, 1972

It was with the recording of this album, apparently, that Michael, now a 14-year-old veteran, began to make it plain that he was less than enchanted with the dictatorial

"I think that to start early is the best way in any field of endeavour. I just thank God for the talent."

 SUGAR DADDY
Out of 'I Want You Back', filtered through 'Mama's Pearl'. They're chasing girls after school again as The Corporation make use of metaphors from the confectionery department – "got a sweet tooth for your love" and so on – plus other well-tried signatures, such as spelled out words and easy, schoolyard rhymes. As a single, its flip 'I'm So Happy' was sung by Jermaine.

manner of production by The Corporation, and others, at Motown. He wanted more freedom to interpret that material as he felt it. Sales of the group's singles, which had been slipping steadily since that initial heady rush, were further affected by the launch of his solo career.

 AIN'T NOTHING LIKE THE REAL THING
A Nick Ashford/Valerie Simpson Motown staple that had been a hit for Marvin

Gaye and Tammi Terrell. In duet with Jermaine, Michael sings his socks off but the track's suprisingly short.

LOOKIN' THROUGH THE WINDOWS

Written by Clifton Davis, composer of 'Never Can Say Goodbye', 'Windows' starts off with a snappy horn orchestration borrowed from Isaac Hayes' 'Theme For Shaft' but the overlybusy arrangement (James Carmichael) obliterates what was once a very simple and charming melody. It's followed by two filler tracks: 'Don't Let Your Baby Catch You' and 'To Know'.

DOCTOR MY EYES

The 1972 Jackson Browne hit was a UK No 9 for the group in February, 1973. Browne purists will be dismayed not by Michael's lead but the rhythm, which substitutes a jaunty pop perkiness for the smooth yet energised LA rock of Browne's original.

LITTLE BITTY PRETTY ONE

See *Greatest Hits*.

E-NE-ME-NE-MI-NE-MOE

A fairly blatant return to to the 'ABC', '1-2-3' school of pop song writing and likely to cause all manner of political correctness outrage if the rhyme is inappropriately concluded.

IF I HAVE TO MOVE A MOUNTAIN

The flip side of 'Little Bitty Pretty One', written by Freddie Perren, Fonze Mizell, Berry Gordy and Deke Richards, is a mid-tempo ballad of no great merit sung solo by Michael. On this track, and others on the album, one can hear how quickly the group's backing vocals are becoming stylised and shrill.

CHILDREN OF THE LIGHT

Successful enough, to Motown's ears, to become the title track of a later compilation. The album ended with a final filler: 'I Can Only Give You Love'.

SKYWRITER

UK Tamla Motown STML 11231
released June, 1973
CD 530 209-2

By now the cracks – rather large fissures actually – were becoming plainly visible in the relationship between The Jackson 5 camp and the label. In March 1973, perhaps sensing disquiet in the group's ranks emanating from Michael and his father, Berry Gordy registered the name "The Jackson 5" as property of Motown. Gordy's attention had been diverted by his hunger for success at the movie box office. The group was beginning to think about shopping around for a better deal and the accepted wisdom is that, as far as the group's records are concerned, there is nothing to concern us here until a couple of albums into the Epic contract.

While it's true that there is filler and dross in some measure, it's also true that this was an interesting period in Michael Jackson's development in purely physical terms if nothing else – he was shooting up as his voice was edging down and filling out – and as a singer he was occasionally given more freedom within the arrangements. He was also becoming established as a solo singer and Jermaine, now involved with Hazel Gordy, daughter of the label's boss, plays a more prominent role more often as a co-lead singer. This was rarely to Jermaine's advantage. For the album sleeve, they posed in front of a single-prop aircraft dressed in flying jackets, goggles and scarves, jodhpurs

and knee-length boots, and very cold and uncomfortable they look too.

SKYWRITER

The Four Seasons were signed to Motown in the early Seventies and there is something of that group's sound and harmonies in the vocal arrangement of this rockier title track.

HALLELUJAH DAY

Unlike many of the great Motown stars of the Sixties, there was never much gospel in The Jackson 5 sound. Despite its title and a nod to the sacred in the lyric, this Freddie Perren and Christine Yarian song is closer to pop than gospel or soul. The track reached No 20 on the UK pop charts.

THE BOOGIE MAN

That's "boogie man" as spooooky rather than funky. Tempting to see Deke Richards' song as a dry-run for the far-distant 'Thriller' but really it's just a novelty piece.

TOUCH
A Frank Wilson and Pam Sawyer ballad shared by Michael and Jermaine. It was a single for the post-Ross Supremes, sandwiched between 'Nathan Jones' and 'Floy Joy', and didn't do much for them, either.

CORNER OF THE SKY

Showstopper lifted from the Broadway musical *Pippin*, shared by Michael, Jermaine and Jackie. (Motown had a stake in *Pippin*, the musical written by Stephen Schwartz, the man who devised *Godspell*. The Original Cast album of *Pippin* was picked up by Motown and the songs were published by Jobete.)

I CAN'T QUIT YOUR LOVE
Cover of a 1972 single by The Four Tops, written by Kathy Wakefield and Leonard Caston. (The Tops couldn't quit the love but they quit the label very soon after.) From the point of view of personal experience, Michael ought not to have been able to sing this as well as he does.

UPPERMOST

Written by Clifton Davis, who penned 'Never Can Say Goodbye', it's a sneakily attractive track built on burbling drum machine and drawing a more mature, considered performance from Michael.

WORLD OF SUNSHINE

Jermaine-led Marcellino/Larson song again sounding faintly like The Four Seasons.

OOH I'D LOVE TO BE WITH YOU
A Fonce and Larry Mizell song, produced by the Fonce and Freddie Perren, featuring Jermaine and an arrangement leaning towards Timmy Thomas' 'Why Can't We Live Together', which had been a hit in November, 1972.

YOU MADE ME WHAT I AM

How's this for subliminal messages? It's a song to be sung as thanks to their audience, of course, but it's also written, arranged and produced by The Corporation – as in "we made you what you are, boys" and don't forget it. As history shows, they did forget. Of course, the song can also be interpreted as giving thanks to their Lord.

GET IT TOGETHER

UK Tamla Motown STML 11243
released November, 1973

 GET IT TOGETHER
Wow! Within the space of a few months, Michael Jackson's voice takes on a new resonance and strength and he suddenly sounds like a young adult. Fired by a funky keyboard part, Hal Davis' production of Arthur Wright's excellent arrangement catches the full bustle of a close-knit band, a rare artefact indeed in the late-Jackson 5 canon. It was a very promising start to an album with a distinct dance floor bias.

 REFLECTIONS
A Holland-Dozier-Holland hit for The Supremes in 1967 to which The Jackson 5 could add little.

 HUM ALONG AND DANCE
To impressionable young Jackson 5 fans reared on the sanctity of the three-minute single and album track, this James Carmichael-arranged version of the Norman Whitfield/Barrett Strong opus must have come as a fair old shock. It's a lo-o-o-ong workout for the band with a refreshingly honest lyric. There ain't no words to the song, you just dance and hum along, they sing: "Like I said, we didn't have no time to write none."

 MAMA I GOT A BRAND NEW THING (DON'T SAY NO)
Another Whitfield work-out in which the young men from Gary, Indiana have a further stab walking in The Temptations' shoes. Clearly, this was Motown's biggest problem. Now that the group was out-growing its predominantly teen-appeal, the label could not *hear* an individual sound. The writers and producers couldn't get past the teen act and so The Jackson 5 are shoe-

> ## "I'm still amazed at how my voice used to sound. They used to tell me I had the voice of a 35-year-old when it comes to phrasing and control. I have been singing since I was five years old, so by the time I began to make those records, I'd already had five or six years' experience."

 DON'T SAY GOODBYE AGAIN
Of course, it couldn't last. The Philly-influenced arrangement doesn't wholly suit Pam Sawyer/Leon Ware's song.

horned into the styles of vocal groups with whom the writers and producers are most familiar.

 TOO LATE TO CHANGE THE TIME
Arthur Wright arranged three tracks on the album and it's comfortably the best work. Michael was surely given almost

complete freedom to sing this how he felt it. How do we know? It's one of the first times you'll hear that soon-to-be-familiar catch in his voice after he's enunciated a word. As in "too late-uh to change the time". A good Pam Sawyer/Leon Ware song; he does it full justice.

YOU NEED LOVE LIKE I DO (DON'T YOU?)

The third and final Whitfield-Strong song on the album features a shared lead by Michael and Jermaine on the Gladys Knight & The Pips favourite from 1970.

DANCING MACHINE

It must have come as quite a shock to the label when the album provided the group's biggest hit in three years. Since 1971's No 2 hit 'Never Can Say Goodbye', The Jackson 5's 45s had failed to get into single figures in the US charts and after 'Get It Together' had failed to dent, expectations must have been low. But the third Arthur Wright arrangement, TV appearances, and exposure in the discos gives Motown a farewell hit single in 1974, four-and-a-half years after 'I Want You Back' announced them. Full circle. Not surprisingly, the next album was...

reworking the back catalogue, but rarely can they have recycled a track so quickly or used a track on one album as the title track of the follow-up. That, however, is what they did here. Again there is much of interest because the group's age demands more challenging and adult material. Not all of it good, of course, but clear pointers to the future.

I AM LOVE

Like Funkadelic but without the heavy funk or sense of anarchy, it took four to write the song, four to arrange it and two to produce the track. "War and poverty wasn't meant to be," sings Jermaine in the guise of 'Love', "hate is driving me away". Michael enters for a brief quote before a long, hard rock guitar solo and much vamping on funk keyboards. A concept track? As such it's a blueprint for some of the more expansive tracks on The Jacksons' Epic albums, such as *Destiny* and *Triumph,* and, alas, some of the overblown tracks on *Victory.* Released as a (Part 1) single.

DANCING MACHINE

UK Tamla Motown STML 11275
released November, 1974

Motown has never been beneath having nine bites of the cherry when it comes to

WHATEVER YOU GOT, I WANT
Considering James Brown's importance as an influence on Michael Jackson's stage performance, it's slightly surprising that he did no covers of the Godfather's material on record. Too black, perhaps? Here, though, the use of baritone sax is clearly out of Papa's bag.

SHE'S A RHYTHM CHILD
Disco rubbish chock-full of clichés. Those concerned, but mostly writers Hal Davis (also producer), Clarence "Clay" Drayton and Ruth Talmage, should be ashamed. No wonder Michael wanted out.

DANCING MACHINE
See final track on 'Get It Together'.

THE LIFE OF THE PARTY
Dance track – how did you guess? – using the vocal background licks from 'Dancing Machine'. Motown thinks enough of this to reprise it on high-profile re-repackages.

WHAT YOU DON'T KNOW
…"won't hurt you" the song decides above a driving track with a very fair horn arrangement.

IF I DON'T LOVE YOU THIS WAY
A Pam Sawyer and Leon Ware ballad and even on filler productions like this Michael rarely sounds as though he's *not* trying.

IT ALL BEGINS AND ENDS WITH LOVE
A ballad sung by Jermaine. As usual it is easy to pick out Michael's voice in the background vocals.

THE MIRRORS OF MY MIND
Laughable wanna-be-a-concept song totally unsuited to the group. Possibly recorded as a bet? A dare? A favour?

MOVING VIOLATION

UK Tamla Motown STML 11290 released July, 1975

Hard not to find signifiers everywhere. On the album sleeve, the 5 are apprehended after flattening an LA traffic cop with their open-top vintage motor (making good their escape from Motown?). Five of the nine tracks were produced by Brian Holland on behalf of Holland/Dozier/Holland Productions Inc. as one of the great totems of Motown in the Sixties returns to oversee the group that found the label a new audience after the H-D-H hit factory packed up their tools and left. Three of the other four tracks were produced by the familiar Larson/Marcellino pairing, the fourth by Hal Davis. Back on the album sleeve, we see that Michael and Marlon have done their growing and are now much the same height as Jackie, Tito and Jermaine. Michael's Afro is vast. Tito used to be the hat man; Marlon's taken over.

FOREVER CAME TODAY
The build-up is cluttered going on indecipherable, but persevere with the disco remake of The Supremes' 1968 hit, groove on the increasingly familiar bass lines, guitar riff and four-on-the-floor bass drum and what do you think happens? 'Forever' turns into an obvious model for the upbeat portion of Diana Ross' great comeback hit 'Love Hangover'. Was this the ultimate Motown cheek, to remake a Jackson 5 remake into La Ross' reviver?

MOVING VIOLATION

Not for the first time, one of the least impressive tracks on a Jackson 5 album becomes title track.

(YOU WERE MADE) ESPECIALLY FOR ME

Neat poppy sound in a Philly groove – it's not hard to hear why Epic put them with Philadelphia International's Kenny Gamble and Leon Huff. Brian Holland's vocal arranger and sometime co-writer on the album is Michael L Smith, one of a new generation of Motown, and independent, producers.

HONEY LOVE

Another cut that again predates but uses similar riffs to 'Love Hangover', it's essentially a groove with vocal extemporisations.

BODY LANGUAGE (DO THE LOVE DANCE)

Dreadful title. In the days when musicians played "real" instruments, arrangers would do something similar to sampling by writing huge quotes from other songs. Thus here there is a whopping quote from Norman Whitfield's 'War'. All that's missing are the words: "What is it good for? Absolutely nothin'! Sayitagin!"

ALL I DO IS THINK OF YOU

A Smith/Holland ballad not to be confused with Stevie Wonder's 'All I Do', very well sung, a maturer ballad sound.

BREEZY

Flimsy would have been a better title for this Larson/Marcellino filler. Jermaine features.

CALL OF THE WILD

Another Larson/Marcellino filler, nothing to do with the Jack London book.

TIME EXPLOSION

A *Phantom Of The Opera* type opening on organ and a track that sounds oddly like a late-Sixties pop attempt. The last three tracks on the album have the definite feel of "Here's another one we found in the piano stool!"

JOYFUL JUKEBOX MUSIC

UK Motown STML 12046
released December, 1976

Released after four-fifths of the original group had gone to Epic, a collection of out-takes with very few highlights. One can only think it was released to show the group at its worst and ruin what reputation they had after waning singles and album sales and the ugly split with their label and brother Jermaine. Obviously, it was released as a spoiler to The Jacksons' Epic début. (Another spoiler, released across the Pond on Motown's Natural Resources label, was titled *Boogie*. Many of the tracks later turned up on the 1986 compilation *Looking Back To Yesterday*.)

JOYFUL JUKEBOX MUSIC
A dreadful, grinning, stiff-limbed rock'n'roller, namechecking The Beatles and the Stones, sounding like something put together for a Las Vegas stage show.

WINDOW SHOPPING
Uptempo, with a Philly influence.

YOU'RE MY BEST FRIEND, MY LOVE
A happy, mid-tempo sound provided by this Philly arrangement. One can imagine Michael singing this to his menagerie.

LOVE IS THE THING YOU NEED
An old sound, with Michael sounding two or three years younger.

THE ETERNAL LIGHT
The electric piano introduction doesn't prepare one for the surprise track of the album – a good song. Larson/Marcellino wrote and produced it, James Carmichael arranged it. The finished product has a Southern soul feel, almost totally unheard of in the great majority of the Motown catalogue, certainly there's nothing like it in The Jackson 5 catalogue to prepare one for it. The horns are Stax influenced. Somewhat spiritual, too. "Let's try to show compassion... there's a lot for us to learn."

PRIDE AND JOY
A remake of Marvin Gaye's 1963 hit and considerably more adventurous than the usual re-styling as the soul shuffle is turned into rippling keyboard-based funk.

THROUGH THICK AND THIN
Mid-tempo pop tune with Jermaine singing straight man role to Michael's more distinctive co-lead.

WE'RE HERE TO ENTERTAIN YOU
Further proof that Michael has the bornperformer's ability to sing the corniest rubbish with absolute conviction. When they were tiny little boys, he sings, they used to dance and sing before they could... well, I'm sure you catch the drift. As they grew up, they didn't change, knew they liked the spotlight and the stage. Actually, for Michael this *is* autobiography so no wonder he sings it with belief. As with the title track, it sounds like a page out of their Las Vegas songbook.

MAKE TONIGHT ALL MINE
Filler, true, but a jolly filler.

WE'RE GONNA CHANGE OUR STYLE

Nice touch to end their Motown career on a song so titled. Unfortunately, it is a clattering, muddled noise and not very good. Sour grapes rather than a fond farewell.

In addition to the first Greatest Hits package, which is still good value as a cheap, concise introduction to the group's work, there have been many other compilations, such as *20 Golden Greats* (STML 12121).

One interesting idea was their contribution to the 'Motown Special' series (STMX 6006) in which the 11 songs combined three of their own hits with their versions of songs made popular by Motown acts such as The Temptations, Stevie Wonder, The Miracles and Marvin Gaye, among others. But the best compilations are those in the Motown Anthology series. These combined Jackson 5, Michael Jackson and Jermaine Jackson hits. The series started in the mid-Seventies with a double album, grew to a double CD and by the late-Eighties had become a four CD boxed set priced at around the £40 mark.

ANTHOLOGY

UK Motown TMSP 6004
January, 1977
CD WD 72529

The first *Anthology* double album, compiled in rough chronological order, had 19 tracks by the 5, nine by Michael and two from Jermaine. When re-released in 1981 it had three fewer tracks. The original listing is: –

'I Want You Back', 'ABC', 'The Love You Save', 'I'll Be There', 'Mama's Pearl', 'Never Can Say Goodbye', 'Got To Be There' (Michael Jackson), 'Sugar Daddy', 'Rockin' Robin' (Michael Jackson), 'Little Bitty Pretty One', 'I Wanna Be Where You Are' (Michael Jackson), 'Ain't No Sunshine' (Michael Jackson), 'Lookin' Through The Windows', 'Ben' (Michael Jackson), 'That's How Love Goes' (Jermaine Jackson), 'Doctor My Eyes', 'Daddy's Home' (Jermaine Jackson), 'Hallelujah Day', 'Morning Glow' (Michael Jackson), 'Skywriter', 'Get It Together', 'The Boogie Man', 'Music And Me' (Michael Jackson), 'The Life Of the Party', 'Dancing Machine', 'Whatever You Got', 'I Want', 'We're Almost There' (Michael Jackson), 'I Am Love', 'Forever Came Today', 'Just A Little Bit Of You' (Michael Jackson).

SOULSATION! MICHAEL JACKSON WITH THE JACKSON FIVE

Motown
CD 530 489-2

Four-CD boxed set in the Motown Master Series, part of the 25th anniversary collection, with a well-illustrated 68-page booklet, essay by David Ritz (biographer of Marvin Gaye and Ray Charles, among others). Expensive but not unrewarding package. The fourth CD has "Rare and Unreleased" tracks.

CD1: I Want You Back, Who's Lovin' You, You've Changed, Stand!, Can You Remember, ABC, The Love You Save, I Found That Girl, La La (Means I Love You), I'll Bet You, (Come 'Round Here) I'm The One You Need, The Young Folks, I'll Be There, Goin' Back To Indiana, Can I See You In The Morning, Mama's Pearl, Reach In, Christmas Won't Be The Same This Year, Santa Claus Is Coming To Town, Never Can Say Goodbye, Maybe Tomorrow, She's Good.

CD2: Got To Be There (Michael), People Make The World Go 'Round (Michael), Teenage Symphony, Sugar Daddy, Ain't Nothin' Like The Real Thing, Lookin' Through The Windows, Doctor My Eyes, Little Bitty Pretty One, If I Have To Move A Mountain, Rockin' Robin (Michael), I Wanna Be Where You Are (Michael), Ben (Michael), Skywriter, You Made Me What I Am, Hallelujah Day, Touch, Corner Of The Sky, The Boogie Man, Get It Together, Dancing Machine, It's Too Late To Change The Time, Whatever You Got, I Want.

Jermaine, Jackie, basketball player Elgin Baylor & Michael

"I'll tell you the honest-to-God truth. I never knew what I was doing in the early days – I just did it. I never knew how I sang, I didn't really control it, it just formed itself."

CD3: The Life Of The Party, I Am Love Pts I & II, If I Don't Love You This Way, Mama I Gotta A Brand New Thing (Don't Say No), Forever Came Today, Body Language (Do The Love Dance), All I Do Is Think Of You, It's A Moving Violation, (You Were Made) Especially For Me, Honey Love, That's How Love Goes (Jermaine), Daddy's Home (Jermaine), Just A Little Bit Of You (Michael), Love Is The Thing You Need, The Eternal Light, Pride And Joy, You're My Best Friend, My Love, Joyful Jukebox Music, Love Don't Want To Leave (Jackie).

CD4: Can't Get Ready For Losing You, You Ain't Giving Me What I Want (So I'm Taking It All Back), Reach Out I'll Be There, I'm Glad It Rained, A Fool For You, It's Your Thing, Everybody Is A Star, I Need You (Jermaine), You're The Only One, Just A Little Misunderstanding, Jamie, Ask The Lonely, We Can Have Fun, I Hear A Symphony, Let's Have A Party, Love Scenes, LuLu, Money Honey, Coming Home.

PART II
MICHAEL JACKSON: SOLO AT MOTOWN

By 1972, if not before, it was obvious that although in young girls' hearts Jermaine Jackson was the 5's pin-up and received a larger share of fan mail, Michael had by far the better voice. It was rangier, he had better control over it, the pitch was certain and he had much the greater capacity for expression. Add to this his ability to learn quickly and willingly and an appetite for work bordering on gluttony and you have a piece of clay primed for moulding.

His "solo" career at Motown essentially consisted of four albums – *Got To Be There, Ben, Music & Me* and *Forever Michael.* When he left – dismayed by falling record sales and Motown's refusal to let the group write its own material – a steady deluge of repackages followed.

GOT TO BE THERE

UK Tamla Motown STML 11205
released April, 1972
CD 530 162-2

In *Moonwalk*, Jackson said in 1972, when he was 14, around the time of the *Lookin' Through The Windows* album, he started to question producers' insistence that he sing a song in a certain way. He thinks, he wrote, that Gordy told producers to give him more freedom. It was at this time, also, that he had a growing spurt and ceased to be the cheeky-looking boychild Michael, and turned into a stick-limbed teenager with a bad case of acne. This is mortifying enough when you're just a kid on the block but for a youth who's up on stage, centre of attention in the

Diana Ross had detached herself from The Supremes, Smokey Robinson was embarking on a post-Miracles career, David Ruffin and, soon, Eddie Kendricks were out of The Temptations. Another great lead voice, Levi Stubbs, had with The Four Tops left

"I used to come home from school at three and everything would be set up in the living room, the drums and all, and we practised until night and we kept on and kept on and we had meetings and we used to wonder, 'When will we have a show?'"

biggest teen sensation of the decade, it verged on the emotionally crippling. The out-going 12-year-old became a shy and embarrassed 14-year-old. But by this time, he had a solo recording career as well as the group's hits to sustain on and offstage.

the label entirely and very shortly yet another, Gladys Knight, would be on her way with The Pips. Marvin Gaye had been fighting to get a release for 'What's Going On', one of post-war popular music's greatest and most influential achievements, which Gordy thought was a huge mistake, and Stevie Wonder had been locked in contract dispute. All this in the space of a couple of years at the start of the Seventies. No wonder The Jackson 5 were so popular with Gordy. They must have seemed to be the only problem-free good-news zone around. While the group was on a roll, he decided Michael should make a solo single and album. The cheery, smiling face with its bushy Afro flattened by a large cap from the Dickensian props room belongs to a boy who hasn't a care in the world.

AIN'T NO SUNSHINE

Bill Withers' composition had won the Grammy for Best Rhythm & Blues Song in 1971, beating, among others, Clifton Davis' 'Never Can Say Goodbye'. Opening with a monologue, Jackson gives a nicely pitched and well-modulated vocal. Released as a UK single only and reached No 8.

I WANNA BE WHERE YOU ARE

The third single off the album, more "up" in feel than the moody opening track and aptly positioned to illustrate his growing versatility. In the UK, it was the flip of 'Ain't No Sunshine'. It was co-written by Leon Ware and Arthur "T-Boy" Ross, Diana's brother.

GIRL, DON'T TAKE YOUR LOVE FROM ME

Good track. A Willie Hutch song, a Gene Page arrangement, he's supported by good background vocals although the mid-track monologue, on which he sounds a tad too young to be convincing, nearly ruins it.

IN OUR SMALL WAY

Today, says Michael in another opening monologue, we can all change the world in our own small way. Having a 13-year-old grasp philosophical, moral and metaphysical nettles is fraught with danger. In the early Seventies, ecology was then a new, hip concern while brotherly love had become a flawed concept thanks to the Vietnam war and the failure of peaceful protest and demonstration to deliver much in the way of equal opportunity, unless it was to die for your country. But we all can change the world, he sings, in our own small way.

GOT TO BE THERE

The first solo single, written by Elliot Willensky, released in October, 1971, features the sweet, beseeching, multi-tracked voice soaring clear and strong. The mix of gentle, almost wistful longing at the start of couplets that will end on an impossibly high-flying note on key words like "home" and "me" is a real test. The single reached No 4 on the pop and R&B charts in the US and No 5 in the UK.

ROCKIN' ROBIN

The Bobby Day hit from 1958 did not have much in the way of lyric but its beat and melody snapped together to create an infectiously chirpy atmosphere. It was the second solo single and went to No 2 on the US pop and R&B charts.

WINGS OF MY LOVE
In the early part of The Jackson 5 career, there is a suspicion that the young singers were given certain songs by The Corporation because everyone else at Motown had refused to sing them. This is one such.

MARIA (YOU WERE THE ONLY ONE)

The flip side of 'Got To Be There' was given a solidly Four Tops arrangement by James Carmichael. Despite the change of pace halfway through, Michael's voice sounds a little too thin and on the verge of shouting the lyric.

LOVE IS HERE AND NOW YOU'RE GONE
The Holland-Dozier-Holland song that wafted waves of self-pity from the lips of The Supremes in 1967. Jackson sings it with great spirit verging on anger – he sounds really pissed that his girlfriend's made off. It was the flip side of his second single.

YOU'VE GOT A FRIEND

The aforesaid Grammy awards (see 'Ain't No Sunshine') were dominated by Carole King who won four including Song Of The Year for this composition, which also won James Taylor Best Pop Vocal Performance, Male. Michael's reading does not find a lot in the song that is new.

BEN

*UK Tamla Motown STML11220
released December, 1972.
CD 530 163-2*

It is hard to shake off the feeling that the material for Jackson's first three solo albums was recorded at one or two marathon sessions with arrangers and musicians working round the clock, on rotation, in a Herculean effort to get as much material into the can before Michael's voice changed. Certainly there is a homogeneity about the tracks on his first three albums that make them, if not entirely interchangeable, then closely related to the point of inbreeding. *Ben* was a No 5 pop album.

BEN

There are few better-known films that no-one has ever seen than *Ben*, sequel to a similarly rat-infested movie called *Willard*. It was a mild horror-cum-buddy flick in which a boy befriends the rat of the title and wreaks dread revenge on those who would persecute and ridicule him and his rodent chum. Or something like that.

Fortunately, all such nastiness is omitted from the title song, written by Walter Scharf and Don Black. It's a gentle, quite plaintive tune with a lyric about friendship and devotion.

The original album sleeve had a raggle-taggle posse of rats superimposed on a happy snap of Michael, an image bound to send kids to bed screaming. The sleeve was sensibly withdrawn to become, like all shockers, "a collector's item". As a single, 'Ben' was Michael Jackson's first No 1 US pop hit and sold over a million. It was also nominated for Best Song at the Academy Awards but failed to win, and not because he went to the Oscar awards ceremony to sing it live.

GREATEST SHOW ON EARTH

...which is love, apparently, and not Barnum & Bailey's circus, which was probably closer to Michael's heart when he recorded this song. It is, again, a track that shows the label's producers not entirely getting to grips with his talent but merely turning out quick product for the perceived market.

PEOPLE MAKE THE WORLD GO ROUND

The Thom Bell and Linda Creed song that was a hit for The Stylistics is produced here by Hal Davis. After a brief nod to the problems of the world – from industrial strife to eco-doom – we're relieved to know that it's people who make the world go round, the solution is in our own hands (cf 'In Our Small Way' on 'Got To Be There')

WE'VE GOT A GOOD THING GOING

Written and produced by The Corporation, and later a hit as a reggae remake, this catchy pop melody appeared as the B-side of 'I Wanna Be Where You Are'. Would probably have worked better as a Jackson 5 track.

EVERYBODY'S SOMEBODY'S FOOL

Pop-country singer Connie Francis'

version of this song actually made the R&B charts in 1960. Michael's too-stagey cover becomes a one-dimensional shout because the raw material was not suited to his young voice.

MY GIRL

Most every singer has a shot at what is arguably Smokey Robinson's best-loved song, made famous by The Temptations and Otis Redding, and Michael's attempt, stitched together by some neat guitar parts, is a likeably upbeat version.

WHAT GOES AROUND COMES AROUND

In which the singer finds an outlet for the confusions of puberty by revealing a mean streak, revelling in the misfortune of a girl who'd forsaken him and is now herself forsook.

IN OUR SMALL WAY

The track from 'Got To Be There' too hurriedly reprised.

SHOO-BE-DOO-BE-DOO-DA-DAY

Stevie Wonder's piece of fluff from 1968. Michael follows the former Motown child star's vocal closely, which he did more often than one might expect when covering the label's old hits.

YOU CAN CRY ON MY SHOULDER

A good version of an old Berry Gordy song about bringing comfort to someone hurt in love. His shout at the end – "Yes you can *girl!*" is right out of the Levi Stubbs phrasebook. He'd also used it in 'I'll Be There'.

MUSIC & ME

UK Tamla Motown STML 11235
released July, 1973
Spectrum 550 078-2

WITH A CHILD'S HEART

Sounds yucky but this gentle and reflective ballad seems in tune with many of his later pronouncements. With a child's heart, nothing can get you down – it's a reminiscence of innocence to which he will return. Here, he sings, there are no adult thoughts to lead a heart astray. He then proceeds to sing a collection of songs that frankly seem too adult for him.

UP AGAIN

"Up" being the operative word as an optimistic lyric finds a perky melody with hooks picked out by calliope.

Michael & Randy Jackson

ALL THE THINGS YOU ARE

Jerome Kern and Oscar Hammerstein standard given an uptempo disco arrangement by James Carmichael in a Mel Larson/Jerry Marcellino production. It did not sound too clever at the time and is horribly dated now. Michael, to his credit, sings it as though he is at the dentist's – a painful experience to be got through as quickly as possible and in one sitting if you please.

JOHNNY RAVEN

Uptempo track with, towards the end, a romping vocal background. But this child is "born to be wild"? – who's kidding who?

EUPHORIA

In a strangely old-fashioned concept, 'Euphoria' is the word for the new age (Aquarius has dawned and set again, presumably) and Michael spells it out

> ## "[The first gig] was in a shopping centre, the Big Top, in Gary. It was a grand opening. All the people come round to buy the season's fashions. We agreed to be in front of the mall, in the middle of it, and sing. I was about six. I got started around five."

HAPPY

The 'Love Theme' from Diana Ross' movie début as Billie Holiday in *Lady Sings The Blues*, 'Happy' was co-written by Michel Legrand and Smokey Robinson. Gene Page arranged here; Hal Davis produced. Again, Michael sings it straight and brings very little of himself to it.

TOO YOUNG

Compared to Nat King Cole's silken tone, Michael's piping voice gives utter credence to the song's title. He does indeed seem much too young to sing the song, let alone fall in love.

DOGGIN' AROUND

Berry Gordy was a big Jackie Wilson fan and wrote many of his early hits but not this one. It was one of Wilson's bluesier tracks, a double-sided hit, with 'Night', in 1960. Unsurprisingly, Michael's version sounds like a kid imitating an adult, which is what it was. That said, it's a good piece of mimicry.

for us – "E-U-P-H... O-R-I-A" – which is a considerable improvement on 'ABC'. If you're lucky to be living in the land of euphoria you'll be happy to be living the way you choose. Possibly one of the first "E" songs ever recorded.

MORNING GLOW

Another track from the Broadway show *Pippin* (see 'Corner Of The Sky' on 'Skywriter'). Produced by Bob Gaudio, best known for his work with The Four Seasons. There is a whiff of Joni Mitchell in the melody.

MUSIC AND ME

Like the album's first track, this personal reflection – "we've been together for such a long time, my music and me" – written for him by four other writers, can only have hardened his resolve to create his own songs. The piece creates a mood similar to 'Ben'.

FOREVER, MICHAEL

UK Tamla Motown STMA 8022
released February, 1975
CD WD 72121

Solo equivalent of The Jackson 5's roughly contemporaneous *Moving Violation* album – which means under-rated with tougher dance tracks and an appreciably more mature lead vocalist who does indeed sound like a Young Man as opposed to a growing kid. There are further tracks here produced by Brian Holland good enough to wish he, co-writer Eddie Holland and Michael had been given the opportunity to work on a whole album. But by now, the brother from Gary, Indiana, had had his fill of Motown production mores, had learnt all he could and needed to write and produce his own material.

WE'RE ALMOST THERE
The first of three Brian and Eddie Holland compositions on the album. Michael's voice immediately sounds *older*. There's a quiver of emotion in it, a slightly rasping edge. The voices that spring to mind as most comparable are Gladys Knight and Candi Staton.

TAKE ME BACK
Michael sings this second Holland brothers' song with an expression and freedom that, by comparison with his early studies of other singers' styles, verges on the abandoned.

Diana Ross & Michael

ONE DAY IN YOUR LIFE
This mawkish ballad is a theme song looking for its movie as the deserted young lover declares undying loyalty. He will stay in her heart and, when she is in need, she'll remember him and he'll come a-running. Michael sings it nicely and it was a hit for Motown long after he'd quit the label, his first ever solo No 1 in the UK, in fact.

CINDERELLA STAY AWHILE
Hard to know who was going through the motions the most – the writers, arranger David Blumberg, producer Hal Davis or Michael.

WE'VE GOT FOREVER
Little did they know. Sung as a duet with himself, a love song promising music and each other until a minute after the end of time.

1958
AUGUST 29

Michael Joseph Jackson is the seventh child born to Katherine and Joe Jackson in Gary, Indiana.

1969

'I Want You Back'/'Who's Loving You', the Jackson 5's début single is released on Motown Records and sells two million copies in six weeks.

1970

The Jackson 5 reach sales of ten million worldwide for the singles 'I Want You Back,' 'ABC' and 'The Love You Save' during a nine-month period - a record unsurpassed in such a time period.

1970

'ABC' hits number 1 on the Pop singles chart, replacing The Beatles' 'Let It Be',

1972

'Got To Be There', Michael's first solo single, released.

Off The Wall, Michael's first solo LP on which he has full creative control, is released.

1978

Destiny, the first Jacksons album on Epic is released

1975

The Jackson 5, including Michael, announce they have signed with Epic Records. Because Jermaine Jackson, who is married to Berry Gordy's daughter, remains with Motown, the group is renamed The Jacksons.

1983

While singles from *Thriller*, including 'Billie Jean', 'Beat It' and the title track, are huge hits across the globe, Michael debuts his moonwalk dance at during a TV show that celebrates Motown's 25th Anniversary.

1982

Michael's *Thriller*, which will go on to become the biggest selling album on all time, is released.

1989

Michael is on the cover of *Vanity Fair* magazine, with a picture taken by Annie Leibovitz.

1987

Bad, Michael's third and final album produced by Quincy Jones, is released.

1991

Michael's *Dangerous* album is released.

1991

Michael re-signs his contract with Sony Music which had bought CBS in 1988. It is reported to be the biggest music deal in history.

1994

Michael marries Elvis Presley's daughter, Lisa Marie, in the Dominican Republic.

1997

Debbie Rowe gives birth to
Michael's son Prince Michael
in Los Angeles.

1998

Michael's wife
Debbie Rowe gives
birth to a baby girl,
Paris Michael
Katherine Jackson.

2001

Michael's album, *Invincible*, is released.

2008

Celebrating the 25th anniversary of Thriller, *Thriller 25* is released, containing remixes and a previously unreleased song.

To celebrate Jackson's 50th birthday in August, Sony BMG released a compilation album.

2009
JUNE 25

Michael dies from a heart attack at a rented home in Los Angeles.

JUST A LITTLE BIT OF YOU

The third Brian Holland production on *Forever Michael,* all of which make it a set worth hearing. A strong horn section introduction and, if the rhythm section had been mixed with a touch more kick, the track would have been in real business. Just a little bit of you, he sings, will surely keep the doctors away. Hey, it beats an apple a day. The lyric doesn't amount to much but, immunised or not, it's a very infectious track.

YOU ARE THERE

As opposed to 'Got To Be There'? The ballad is sung against accompaniment tailored for that sweet soul territory where The Chi-Lite meets The Stylistics.

DAPPER DAN

A role-playing narrative in which he's a "little country boy", neat with the harmonica and blessed with the fastest feet around. "Do-it, do-it" they chant, "let me show you" he sings. Years later, he did. Despite the energy and superficial enthusiasm, there's a half-hearted air about the track.

DEAR MICHAEL

Although he didn't write it, how's about this for a dissection of pre-'Billie Jean' attitude to fans. In this Hal Davis/Elliot Willensky song, he imagines a fan writing to him about her desire to be more than just a fan (didn't they all?). The moving letter touches his heart, he promises to reply. "Hurry Mr Postman, deliver my letter." Already he's living deep inside his own career and getting a sense of being trapped by the adulation and demands on his emotions.

I'LL COME HOME TO YOU

A mid-tempo 'lurve' ballad and not much to it. A disappointing end.

THE BEST OF...

UK Tamla Motown STML 12005
released September, 1975
WD 72063

Safe and predictable 14-song collection from the four previous albums. It has been re-released several times under new catalogue series numbers. Tracks: 'Got To Be There', 'Ain't No Sunshine', 'My Girl', 'Ben', 'Greatest Show On Earth', 'I Wanna Be Where You Are, Happy (Love Theme From *Lady Sings The Blues*)', 'Rockin' Robin', 'Just A Little Bit Of You', 'One Day In Your Life', 'Music And Me', 'In Our Small Way', 'We're Almost There', 'Morning Glow'.

And with the departure to Epic of Michael, Marlon, Jackie, Tito and Randy, who had replaced Jermaine, you might have been forgiven for thinking "That's All Folks" as far as Motown recordings were concerned. In fact there have been more Michael Jackson solo albums on Motown since he left the label than when he was part of Gordy's empire. Broadly speaking, these came in four disguises:

1. "Concept" compilations such as *The Great Love Songs Of...* (there was also a Jackson 5 album in the series) and *The Original Soul Of Michael Jackson,* which went for a certain style, and more straightforward Michael Jackson & The Jackson 5 Greatest Hits packages with 14, 16 or 18 tracks, depending on the format. All of these relied on the comfort and familiarity of previously available, well-known tracks. Here is an example:

THE GREAT LOVE SONGS OF MICHAEL JACKSON

European Motown WL 72289
released November, 1984
CD WD 72289

In a low-key sell, there was not even a shot of the singer on the album sleeve. Tracks: 'Got To Be There', 'I Wanna Be Where You Are', 'In Our Small Way', 'Girl Don't Take Your Love From Me', 'Maria (You Were The Only One)', 'Love Is Here And Now You're Gone', 'Happy (Love Theme From *Lady Sings The Blues*)', 'I'll Come Home To You', 'You Are There', 'One Day In Your Life'.

2. Albums that use celebration of the label's past to launch a series such as the 'Superstar Series' (Michael was Superstar number seven in the Motown firmament, The Jackson 5 were number 12), which was

pithily titled 'Great Songs & Performances That Inspired The Motown 25th Anniversary TV Show'. There was a combined Michael Jackson and Jackson 5 set in this 1983 series but in 'The Motown Legends' it was The Jackson 5 featuring Michael Jackson. All of these are, at best, partial histories, although collectors find some of them interesting.

SUPERSTAR SERIES VOLUME 7

US Motown M5107V1
released August, 1980

With a cover shot of a very young Michael J, tracks are: 'One Day In Your Life', 'Ben', 'Take Me Back', 'Just A Little Bit Of You', 'I Wanna Be Where You Are', 'We're Almost There', 'Cinderella Stay Awhile', 'Got To Be There', 'Rockin' Robin', 'With A Child's Heart'.

> "We were doing a theatre in Chicago called the Regal, which was kind of an audition for Motown. Since Diana Ross was the hottest act at the time, they decided to use her name to introduce us to the public."

put together in 1980 to celebrate the label's 20th anniversary. Strangely, the label celebrated its 25th anniversary only three years later with another series of albums

3. The third type of compilation hits the rack when an old album track or single that flopped is suddenly picked up or re-promoted, apparently on a whim. But usually

did have two that the UK album didn't – 'We've Got Forever' and 'Make Tonight All Mine'.)

4. The fourth strand of compilation albums comprises those unreleased recordings that Motown had by the shelf-full on many of its major artists. (The Jackson 5 recorded an estimated 70 tracks during their first year in Hollywood; between 30 and 40 before the first record was released.) Very, very occasionally, Motown hit paydirt with this old material. Although most of The Jackson 5 and Michael Jackson's Motown work was done in Los Angeles some masters ended up in Detroit and among a 40-song batch that was lost in the move to the West Coast but rediscovered much later was 'Farewell My Summer Love', a No 38 pop hit in the US but in the UK it sold as easy as ABC and rose to No 7. Here are two albums with "never before released" splashed across the cover.

there has been some market research or some club play or a radio dee-jay gets a bee in his or her bonnet. Anyway, the record becomes a hit and the company slaps together a quick cash-in album. Hence, 'One Day In Your Life', a flop in the UK in 1975, found fresh legs in 1981…

ONE DAY IN YOUR LIFE

UK Tamla Motown STML 12158
released 1981

Tracks: 'One Day In Your Life', 'We're Almost There', 'You're My Best Friend', 'My Love', 'Don't Say Goodbye Again', 'Take Me Back', 'It's Too Late To Change The Time', 'We've Got A Good Thing Going', 'You Are There', 'Doggin' Around', 'Dear Michael', 'Girl Don't Take Your Love From Me', 'I'll Come Home To You'. (The US album had only 10 tracks but

FAREWELL MY SUMMER LOVE

Europe Motown ZL72227
released June, 1984
CD WD 72630

Originally, the album's title had 1984 appended but this was soon dropped. The subtitle reads: "Never before available… from the platinum vaults of Motown". Here's what they found in those vaults. The tracks were recorded in 1973 and new overdubs and mixes were added by Michael Lovesmith (keyboards), Mike Baird (drums),

Tony Peluso, (guitar) and Steve Barri (percussion) with engineer Peluso co-producing with Lovesmith and Barri. At one point, the sleeve notes make a brave attempt to argue that the tracks are some kind of missing link between Sixties soul and the Michael Jackson of *Off The Wall* and *Thriller* and that Al Green was a major stylistic influence on Michael, the latter an even more far-fetched theory than the former. Around this time, Michael would have been recording material for Jackson 5 albums *Get It Together* and possibly *Skywriter* and for *Music And Me,* although he sounds slightly older here.

DON'T LET IT GET YOU DOWN

A prominent rock guitar intro, funkier drums than might be expected in August, '73, beefed up background vocals and horns on a Mel Larson/Jerry Marcellino production (they co-wrote with The Corporation connection Deke Richards) that was likely rejected from *Get It Together.*

YOU'VE REALLY GOT A HOLD ON ME

A remake of the Smokey Robinson classic, Michael sounds "between" voices. That is, the piping kid has gone but the more assured high tenor sounds a semi-tone away. Emotionally, his reading of the lyric doesn't quite convince one that his girl's *really* got a hold on him. First recorded in June, 1973 as was...

MELODIE

Typical of the way Motown had young Michael singing about love. He could not, of course, sing of the squelchy, gristly part of love – The Daughters Of The American Revolution would be smashing records outside the company's offices for feeding impure thoughts to the Granddaughters Of the American Revolution. So love, as in this Larson/Marcellino/Richards song, has to affect him in an old-fashioned, moon-June way that makes him want to sing with joy on this beautiful morning. Oh happy day.

TOUCH THE ONE YOU LOVE

Or maybe he could sing about the grippy, grabby, sweaty stuff. Touch the one you love, advises this George Clinton/Artie Wayne song recorded in June 1973, if you want the one you love to touch you. Quite good. Clinton's vocal group, The Parliaments, were signed to Motown for a few years in the Sixties although nothing was ever released by them.

GIRL, YOU'RE SO TOGETHER

Keni Lewis, who wrote 'Farewell My Summer Love', also penned this frothy love song in which 'honey bees' make an appearance. The piece of fluff was recorded in August 1973.

FAREWELL MY SUMMER LOVE

The album's *raison d'être* is a summer holiday romancer that struck a chord with anyone who ever met someone on holiday, had that fling and promised to write, phone and be faithful until same time-same paddling pool next year. In other words, the kind of holiday promise that lasts for no more than two-and-a-half weeks when you get home. He sings it nicely and the four-on-the-floor drumming kicks the track along.

CALL ON ME

Again in the cloak of a swain whose girl has gone to another while he's left behind providing that safe haven, shoulder to cry on and so forth. Recorded September, 1973.

HERE I AM
(COME AND TAKE ME)

An utterly disastrous cover of the Al Green hit. Hard to think of a less convincing or appealing Michael Jackson vocal performance.

TO MAKE MY
FATHER PROUD

In the light of what we now know of life at home in Gary, Indiana, and the rather unforgiving regime instituted by Joe Jackson, there is some irony in this song, which was produced and co-written by Bob Crewe, The Four Seasons' producer/writer. Very Italian, a mandolin picks out a refrain and a heavenly choir stands by. The title line is completed by "and to make my mother smile". Hey, he's a gooda boy, dat Michael.

LOOKING BACK
TO YESTERDAY

European Motown WL 72424
released May, 1986

To judge by his voice, this archive material dates from 1970/71, certainly earlier than the masters to 'Summer Love'. To emphasise the point, there's a shot of Michael looking *really* young on the sleeve. A familiar mixture of originals and covers, some of them recorded as part of The Jackson 5. The sleeve note suggests these nuggets were held back because the market was already flooded with Jackson product and, to describe Michael's talent, here uses the word "mystical" three times in three paragraphs. But it was the producer writing.

WHEN I COME OF AGE

Mid-tempo ballady thing in which Jackson dreams of becoming a movie star, an astronaut, the captain of a ship, rich and famous. Two out of five ain't too bad.

TEENAGE SYMPHONY

Let us all join hands and give thanks that this Jackson 5 "concept" track was not released in the early Seventies. "Music," a voice intones, "is a universal language that everyone can understand" and The Jacksons want to add their voice. Mostly, they give thanks to the inspiration provided by the audience's "sweet vibes".

I HEAR A SYMPHONY

Michael and The Jackson 5 stick to the Holland-Dozier-Holland text as written and produced for The Supremes. (For passion, hear The Isley Brothers' version.)

GIVE ME HALF A CHANCE

Written by Clifton Davis, composer of 'Never Can Say Goodbye', and performed with the 5, Michael gives it his all, but the song lacks 'Goodbye's' ease.

LOVE'S GONE BAD

Interesting choice. Written by Holland-Dozier-Holland and a 1966 hit for Chris Clark, the label's first white woman singer, on the VIP subsidiary. Michael sings it with a bit of Levi Stubbs but the backing singers (it is not, apparently, a 5 track) use Temptations vocal moves.

LONELY TEARDROPS

Another Berry Gordy co-composition written for Jackie Wilson in 1958 before Motown was set up. Not a great version.

YOU'RE GOOD FOR ME

The lead vocal is pulled way forward for this mid-tempo ballad with The Jackson 5. A guitar passage with a Stylistics feel is prominent.

THAT'S WHAT LOVE IS MADE OF

Smokey Robinson songs were well-suited to his voice at this time, witness a straightforward version of The Miracles' 1964 hit.

I LIKE THE WAY YOU ARE (DON'T CHANGE YOUR LOVE ON ME)

A frantically busy chorus with berserk drumming made singing this Willie Hutch song more like an assault course than a plea for constancy.

WHO'S LOOKIN' FOR A LOVER
Possibly recorded a touch later than the rest of the material because his voice is slightly fuller, less piping.

I WAS MADE TO LOVE HER

This Jackson 5 cover of the Stevie Wonder hit is another rarity – the arrangement does not closely follow the original. The song is slowed down from Stevie's joyful full pelt. It is not Michael's voice or interpretation that lets down the project but the playing does by not getting to grips with the desired feel. Played this slow, the music must be *fonky*.

IF'N I WAS GOD

Robert and Richard Sherman are probably best known as the composers of the motion picture score for *Mary Poppins*. They wrote this too, a big show ballad that Michael sings very well. Starts out saying he wouldn't set the sun til everyone was treated right, if'n he was God. Pretty soon, many millions would think he was something close to it.

Michael Jackson at Motown. You also get five Jackson 5 tracks. In the Motown fashion, the accompanying booklet is illustrated with promotional shots from the years before he started having bits snipped off his face and a note that's rock bottom on analysis and criticism. Tracks are:

CD 1 – Got To Be There, Rockin' Robin, Ain't No Sunshine, Maria (You Were The Only One), I Wanna Be Where You Are, Girl Don't Take Your Love From Me, Love Is Here And Now You're Gone, Ben, People Make The World Go Round, Shoo-Be-Doo-Be-Doo-Da-

> ## "We used to do these club shows and there was this one lady – you probably know what she did – but I thought it was awful. I was around six and she was one of those stripteasers, and she would take her drawers off, and a man would come up, and they'd start doing... aw man, she was too funky. Ugh! That, to me, was awful!"

ANTHOLOGY

European Motown CD 530 178-2 released January, 1987

Two-CD set whose 40 tracks provide a good, all-round introduction to the work of young

Day, With A Child's Heart, Everybody's Somebody's Fool, In Our Small Way, All The Things You Are, You Can Cry On My Shoulder, (and with The Jackson 5) Maybe Tomorrow, I'll Be There, Never Can Say Goodbye, It's Too Late To Change The Time, Dancing Machine.

CD-2 – When I Come Of Age, Dear Michael, Music And Me, You Are There, One Day In Your Life, Love's Gone Bad, That's What Love Is Made Of, Who's Looking For A Lover, Lonely Teardrops, We're Almost There, Take Me Back, Just A Little Bit Of You, Melodie, I'll Come Home To You, If 'N I Was God, Happy (Love Theme From *Lady Sings The Blues*), Don't Let It Get You Down, Call On Me, To Make My Father Proud, Farewell My Summer Love.

PART III
THE JACKSONS AT EPIC

One of the greatest motivating factors that drove The Jackson 5 to leave Motown was their desire, Michael's especially, to become more involved in writing and production. It is hard to believe that the label did not see this coming.

In the studio, he had the reputation of being "a sponge" soaking up information all the time. His producers, the engineers, the musicians, must have seen that the long hours he'd put in at the studio, all of the techniques he'd learnt, were creating a volcano of ambition, ready to blow unless it achieved an outlet.

In *Moonwalk,* Michael insisted that he'd been the only brother with the guts to go head-to-head with Berry Gordy and demand an increasing level of autonomy in their career. His brother Jermaine, who stayed at Motown, told a different story. While enjoying success with 'Let's Get Serious' in 1979 (the year Michael was hitting with *Off The Wall),* for a millisecond it looked as though there would be genuine commercial and artistic rivalry here, he told me: "It wasn't my decision to be solo. This is not what I wanted to do. But I had no choice... Usually when

season played at the MGM Grand Hotel, Las Vegas, in the spring of 1974 when the entire progeny of Joe and Kathleen Jackson – the original 5 plus Randy, sisters Maureen (known professionally as "Rebbie"), Janet and La Toya – unveiled a cabaret act in a bid to shake off their teeny-bop image and broaden their market. In some of the photographs posed backstage, Jermaine, looking rather glum, is slightly but perceptibly detached from the rest of the entourage. It is fluent body language.

"My pockets would be loaded with money. Because she would throw money on the stage. We would have around $300 lying on the stage, and we would make just $25 from the manager paying us."

you hear of somebody going someplace else at least you would sit down and have a discussion about it. The first thing I saw was all the contracts with their names on it, so they had already left. They figured by signing ahead of time, I would go ahead and sign." Later in the interview, after launching a vigorous defence of his then father-in-law's label, he said, "To this very day I can say that Michael never wanted to leave. Because he was too young to voice a strong opinion, to say 'No father, I am not going, I am very happy where I am'."

Jermaine said he felt that the group simply panicked when the hits dried up after that phenomenal start. "So when, all of a sudden, that cools off one would probably get nervous and say, 'Well, what's wrong?' And you say, 'Well, the record company's not doing something right so maybe we oughta leave and go elsewhere.' But everybody, they're hot for a while and then they cool off. As big as The Beatles were, they cooled off and split up and had individual success."

One of the more poignant visual images that appears to predict the split came during the

But, split they did. CBS assigned the group, now named The Jacksons after discovering that Gordy had registered The Jackson 5 name as Motown property in 1973, to Epic. It was announced that production would be by Kenny Gamble and Leon Huff, the masters of Philadelphia International Records who had so successfully refined the Philly Sound that it dominated a large share of the R&B/soul market in the Seventies. Their Sigma Sound Studios in Philly became synonymous with Seventies sophisticated soul, just as the Tamla Motown studios in Detroit had been the template for Sixties urban soul. They had a reputation of making hit singles but their albums sold well too – Harold Melvin & The Blue Notes featuring Teddy Pendergrass, The O'Jays and The Intruders among the group's benefitting – and they had more adult ideas, material and sound, which the group needed. Moreover, at Motown, The Jackson 5 had covered many Philly songs (not by Gamble & Huff) that had been hits for groups, notably The Delfonics and The Stylistics. But they had been much the sweeter kind of Philly; Gamble & Huff favoured tougher stuff and were comfortable with singers who could imbue their singing with a real, desperate, sweaty passion, such as Pendergrass and The O'Jays' Eddie Levert. Whether that style would work for the Jacksons was one of the more intriguing questions awaiting an answer. Michael recorded three albums with The Jacksons before resuming his solo recording career and even after he'd struck out alone there would be three more studio albums with his brothers, one of which was as good as any other contemporary pop record.

THE JACKSONS

Epic EPC 86009
released November, 1976
CD release Epic/Pickwick 982738-2

As a spoiler, Tamla Motown had released *The Jackson 5 Anthology* in June (January, 1977 in the UK) and *Joyful Jukebox Music* in October (December in the UK), and much good it did them. The latter was the first Jackson 5 LP to fail to enter the Top 200 albums in the US.

At Sigma, Michael was in "sponge" mode again, absorbing all the advice and hints that Gamble and Huff had to offer about songwriting and production, particularly song construction because the group were also writing material to be considered for inclusion on the album. Compared to the final Jackson 5 albums, this was a great improvement and, in its balance between dance floor, love interest and concern for the moral and physical future of mankind and the planet (a common balance on Gamble & Huff albums), set the pattern for the first

phase of the rest of their lives. The songs here are all very positive and aspirational, in an emotional and spiritual rather than affluent sense. (What more could the wealthy group want?) Simply read the first three song titles to catch the mood: 'Enjoy Yourself', 'Think Happy', 'Good Times'. Life's a breeze! The side finishes with 'Keep On Dancing' and 'Blues Away'. Hard to imagine a more optimistic atmosphere. The songs of the second side veer from personal emotional politics to those of world community.

The vocal sound is a lot more mature and the producers have a better grasp of the possibilities in Michael's voice now that it has changed in range and the tone has taken on richer colours. He is also allowed a deal more leeway in interpreting the lyrics and there is an appreciable increase in the number of vocal devices he throws into the tracks, where appropriate. The absence of Jermaine, the usual vocal foil to Michael, makes it even more apparent that The Jacksons will now gradually, inexorably become The Michael Jackson Group.

Gamble & Huff produced five of the 10 tracks, Dexter Wansel two, Leon McFadden, John Whitehead and Vic Carstarphen one, and on two tracks written by the group, they plus Gamble, Huff, Whitehead, Wansel and McFadden shared cramped credits. While Motown's *Anthology* album reached No 84 on the US pop albums charts and, as mentioned, *Jukebox* stiffed entirely, *The Jacksons* reached No 36.

ENJOY YOURSELF
The first single off the album was a Gamble/Huff song and production that set a steady, 4/4 dance throb. A quasi-dramatic arrangement linked the verses, which basically encouraged a "pretty girl" to relax, let go, enjoy herself riding the rhythm on the dance floor. It was a No 6 US pop hit and No 2 R&B, a No 42 pop hit in the UK but only when it was re-released in March, 1977.

THINK HAPPY

A very full arrangement by Bobby Martin finds room for everything – and a slide guitar. The track is well grounded by a motivating bassline and has several of the standard Philly signatures – the work of the string section, the drummer hitting the open hi-hat and closing it on the next beat to create a "tshh-up, tshh-up" sound, which kicks the rhythm in the chorus. Michael adds the little decorations of gasps and squeals on the end of words that he'd tried at least once on record at Motown…"there ain't no reason-*uh*". The rationale of the Gamble/Huff song is explained by its title.

GOOD TIMES

The pace is slightly slower but the rhythm is every bit as metronomic on the flip side to the album's third single. The melody to this third Gamble/Huff song demands a more reflective performance in order to interpret a lyric that creates a wistful, nostalgic air, all of which is swept aside by…

KEEP ON DANCING

The rhythm to Dexter Wansel's dancer, a simple, hard throb, developed by the 4/4 bass/bass drum track, is more an insistent thud than racing pace until the cut snaps rather suddenly into double-time. Guitar solo and busy keyboards take up the race. The title explains the rest.

BLUES AWAY

Michael's first solo composition on record and the flip side of the album's second single. The optimistic feeling of the track is created by a combination of sunny melody, swaying mid-tempo pace and Michael's voicing of the lyric of recovery. Whether you dance your blues away or go searching for peace somewhere over the rainbow, life will offer you a silver lining and he's it, he suggests.

SHOW YOU THE WAY TO GO

When Motown launched The Jackson 5 in the United States they had four straight No 1 hits. But this, their second single off *The Jacksons,* was the first UK No 1 hit, seven years after the British release of 'I Want You Back'. The fourth Gamble/Huff song on the album has the narrator, Michael, disclaiming omniscience. "But one thing I do know" turns out to be the fact, commonly expressed in pop music, that we must all come together, work together, build together. There is a messianic edge to all of this, as Michael prepares to lead the puzzled, the lost, the bewildered to

a better place where we will all help everyone else to overcome. Thus, he sings, we will get the job done. This is true. Full employment is a wonderful thing and anyone with a problem will forget what it was because they will be too busy helping everyone else. 'Show You' is of a piece with other songs in which Kenny Gamble and Leon Huff express faith in the human race's ability to work out its problems. The ascending chord pattern mirrors the lyric's hope.

 ### LIVING TOGETHER
Fast cut, written, arranged and produced by Dexter Wansel and another "improving" lyric emphasising the bonds of brotherly love, and finding strength in common purpose. Have a good time, the message runs, but that time is running out. Another piece of typical Philly decoration: at the end of every two bars, the last three quaver beats are emphasised, which both draws a line under the previous bars and sets up the next two bars, keeping the music pulsing.

 ### STRENGTH OF ONE MAN
Written and produced by John Whitehead, Gene McFadden and Vic Carstarphen, there is an ill-advised attempt at vocal democracy within the group. We have to be strong, they sing, because the world and our path through it is tough. One of the album's weaker tracks.

 ### DREAMER
There is an unfinished, unresolved quality to this Gamble/Huff song and production, which is probably fair enough because it's about someone just dreaming their life away in search of an unfulfillable and impossibly romantic and idealised kind of love. Tempting to speculate on whether they wrote the song after close observation of 19-year-old Michael Jackson's attitude to relationships at this time.

 ### STYLE OF LIFE
Written by Michael and Tito, the flip side of 'Enjoy Yourself' carried the heavy load of five Philly producers plus all of

The Jacksons which made 10 voices having input. Here is group democracy gone berserk. One of the weaker tracks, it means style of life as in you'd better change it and get in emotional, spiritual and physical shape before it's too late.

GOIN' PLACES

Epic EPC86035
released October, 1976
CD release Epic 468 876-2

In dusty white tie-and-tails, The Jacksons stop at a redneck gas station to ask directions. The album sleeve is suggestive of young men in a hurry on an expedition of discovery. But *Goin' Places* is no more adventurous than a basic refinement on, and improvement of, *The Jacksons*. Nine tracks, two written by the group, five by Gamble & Huff and one each by Whitehead-McFadden-Carstarphen and Wansel-Cynthia Biggs.

Although there is a less obviously messianic feel, we are still on board the Gamble & Huff Love Train. The highs on the album are higher, the lows lower. The rarefied world the group inhabits colours the lyrics of songs like 'Music's Takin' Over' and 'Goin' Places', producing soft solutions (don't worry, think good thoughts, dance the blues away) to hard problems. An interesting point: the choruses are named "singalongs", a rather more accurate description. In the US, the album reached No 63 pop, in the UK No 45.

MUSIC'S TAKIN' OVER

The Whitehead-McFadden-Carstarphen song and third single off the album extols the virtues of music as teacher, psychiatrist, comforter and decision-making tool. It also makes you dance, which is the prime function of this funkier start. With group vocals punctuating more imaginatively, Michael's lead also gives free rein to the vocal mannerism that will become common to his work – the squeezed-out, wrung-out note, the rhythmic grunts and gasps of a man working out at a punchbag. The punchy horn arrangement towards the fade is worth the wait.

GOIN' PLACES

The mind-broadening properties of travel – experience and understanding of other cultures, their customs and traditions – are saluted in a simple song with a good, fast tempo giving the impression of ground covered at speed. The bass guitar, which lays down a part reminiscent of James Jamerson's work at Motown in the Sixties, is in the driving seat. Set up by a rather childish singalong couplet, the lyric neglects to mention that its advice can be taken only by the very rich or those with absolutely no responsibilities. Of course, in reality it's all make-believe. A jolly happy track and the album's first single.

DIFFERENT KIND OF LADY

Written by all five Jacksons, the credits claim, this has the energy and pace of Epic period Michael Jackson solo dancers without their diamond cutting edge. It was the B-side of the second single from the album. The group, and Michael, are working through ideas that will come out later – in fact it is almost like a dry run for 'Shake Your Body (Down To The Ground)' off the next album.

EVEN THOUGH YOU'RE GONE

This Gamble-Huff ballad was the second A-side lifted from the album and looked on the bright side of getting on with life after the break-up of a relationship.

Michael sings it simply and effectively in a mournful, hurt but not mushy or self-pitying performance

JUMP FOR JOY

Dance is recommended as a way of ridding one's mind and body of the cares and woe, the slings and arrows and so forth… It is fortunate to have such a neat track to do the ridding to. The message is: don't value too highly those things that will not get you through the eye of a needle. And don't worry, be happy.

HEAVEN KNOWS I LOVE YOU, GIRL

A monologue leads into Gamble-Huff's song of idealised love. One of the weaker tracks.

MAN OF WAR

All they are saying, is give peace a chance. Now where have I… anyway, anti-war anthems, unless they are spat out with rage against injustice and cruelty, are not especially easy to do convincingly. This one, with vocals shared among the group, sounds a touch naïve in places as though telling a tyrant or despot to desist from genocide will have the desired effect immediately. It was the third single's B-side.

DO WHAT YOU WANNA

The second group composition on the album is not outstanding but the advice – be strong, single-minded and steadfast in what you do – is pretty much the course Michael was mapping out for himself. Coincidentally, make a decision and "stick to it" is the kind of advice Jermaine was getting from Barry White at this time. The track was the B-side of the first single.

FIND ME A GIRL

The final Gamble-Huff ballad. It tells of a lonely boy looking for the idealised girl of his dreams. As regards the emotional credibility of the performance, the vocal sounds like Jackson 5 boys pretending to be men. Not entirely successful.

DESTINY

Epic EPC83200
released December, 1978
CD release CDEPC 32365

'Show You The Way To Go' had certainly shown Michael Jackson and Epic the way forward, and 10 years after his career had been rocketed into orbit he was about to

The third Jacksons album was their first self-production (Epic appointed former Blood Sweat & Tears drummer Bobby Colomby and Mike Atkinson as "executive producers") and the brothers wrote the material as a group except for one track. They pulled in a good studio band – Nathan Watts (bass), rhythm arranger Greg Phillinganes (keyboards), Mike Sembello, Roland Bautista and Paul Jackson (guitars), Ed Green, Rick Marotta or Ricky Lawson (drums) with brothers Tito (guitar) and Randy (congas) – wound it up and let it go.

The album was also the first for Peacock Productions, their newly formed company named after the bird whose colourful plumage "integrates all colours into one, and displays this radiance of fire only when in love". They likened themselves to the peacock by integrating all colours and races through love of music.

"[James Brown] is so magic. I'd be in the wings when I was, like, six or seven, I'd sit there and watch him. He's the most electrifying. He can take an audience anywhere he wants to. The audience just went bananas. He went wild... he gets so out of himself."

be boosted into the stratosphere.
In September, 1977 'Ease On Down The Road', the song featuring Jackson as The Scarecrow in the movie *The Wiz*, Diana Ross' second unsuccessful follow-up to her hit in the Billie Holiday biopic, *Lady Sings The Blues*, was released. Jackson's singing/dancing role, which included the standout performance of 'You Can't Win', was one of the few bright moments in a drab remake of *The Wizard Of Oz*. But through it, Jackson came to work with Quincy Jones, forming the next significant working partnership in his career.

What Michael Jackson might have likened himself to is an overworked – though surely not underpaid – employee of a small thriving company who was its chairman, chief executive, managing director, creative director, production director, marketing director and research and development team. Not yet out of his teens and teased about his skin condition, called "Big Nose" by his less talented brothers, as he alleged in *Moonwalk*, he was also carrying the major burden of the family business, and had been, really, since 1969.

BLAME IT ON THE BOOGIE

You will have heard of folks losing a loved one to another man or woman, or to drink or to gambling. Here, in keeping with the late Seventies obsession, dancing was the aphrodisiac that lured the lover away. In that literal sense it is actually a prescient song – the dance as hardcore drug was still a generation away. It's a good, stomping dance track and Michael's singing is *very* free, especially in the last quarter of the song, using the full panoply of vocal effects that previously he'd used only sparingly. A Top 10 hit as the first single off the album.

PUSH ME AWAY

A lovely wash of melody, breaking like gentle waves on the seashore, sets up this song of broken-hearted insecurity. The dreamer can't square reality with the warmth and love he imagines in his sleep. Sweeping passages of violin, rippling piano notes recreate the tidal feel before Tito's deft guitar solo sets up the final vocal and hope gives way to resignation.

THINGS I DO FOR YOU

Nathan Watts' rocket fuel bass part gives this dance track a funkier feel and drive. Michael sings the title line in unison with his brothers adding "unh", "uh" and "ha" signatures that pick him out in the crowd. Can't miss him. It was released as a single as late as November, 1981 with Michael's solo 'Don't Stop 'Til You Get Enough' on the flip. Clipped drumming, like an Earth, Wind & Fire track, and the increasingly prominent horn arrangement keep the track in perpetual motion leading straight into…

SHAKE YOUR BODY (DOWN TO THE GROUND)

… a swish of hi-hat breaks into another emphatically locomoting bass line this time set up on synthesizer by Phillinganes. This is a disco hymn to the endless dance and builds with wonderfully organic good sense as layers of instrumentation and sound are gradually added. A guitar begins to shadow the bass line, a string section adds chatter, a horn riff speaks up. The increase in excitement is imperceptible at first, but near the end we're climbing walls. Then, much quicker than it was built, the track is dismantled as horns and strings are muzzled, to leave the guitar, drums and bass jammin' on the core riff. Third single off the album, a Top 5 hit.

DESTINY

The Jackson manifesto? An acoustic guitar opening, recalling the introduction to a singer/songwriter's air in the 'Fire And Rain' mould, leads into lyrics that would grace a world-weary concept album. The protagonist is sick of city life and the quest for material things but can't find a way out. (There is something hollow again about wealthy people lecturing the rest on the unsatisfactory nature of the rich life.) However, the music, graduating from lilting verses into tougher choruses, assuages doubts about the lyrics. The increasing light funk aggression in the band's playing reaches a peak with simple guitar solos, the notes spat out in imitation of the narrator's desperation. Not the most obvious choice as second single off the album.

BLESS HIS SOUL

A pretty melody at mid-tempo sung as a duet and a lyric that more than hints at Michael's predicament. He wants to do what's good for him, he sings, but seems to spend his life trying to please others. You've got to make a decision, says the alter-ego voice, make yourself happy. Everyone should cherish you, they say, live for yourself. He's weepy, used and confused, "I give myself at beck and call". It's a perilous life he's living because by trying to please everyone you end up pleasing no-one and a nervous wreck to boot. His life up to 1978?

ALL NIGHT DANCER

… enough of profundity, here is full-pelt dance music attacked with great energy and power. Jacksons dance tracks are all rhythm section, the sweetening is well back in the mix leaving hard-driving drums, pounding bass and busy going on frantic guitars and keyboards to accompany singers who'll dance 'til 5am. Burn this disco down. The flip of the 'Shake Your Body' single.

THAT'S WHAT YOU GET (FOR BEING POLITE)
No prizes for guessing who the character "Jack", pleading for understanding from those about him, is meant to be. Jack is another nice boy who tries hard to give his all, but he's short of love, uncertain and confused about how to get it and give it. It was the flip side of 'Destiny'. (There is an alternative, fictional, reading of the lyric that marks the character "Jack" as a very lonely and repressed creature, one of those who seem vaguely "weird" but you can never put your finger on precisely why until he breaks out as a full-blown psychotic.)

TRIUMPH

Epic EPC 86112
released September, 1980
CD release Epic/Pickwick 986 640-2

By now, *Off The Wall* had been written, arranged, recorded and released to become a great artistic and very considerable commercial success. Michael had taken to heart the subliminal messages from his own songs – those like 'That's What You Get (For Being Polite)' and 'Push Me Away' – and taken full and absolute control of his career, he said, by sacking his father as manager in 1979. He is also much more frugal with his use of vocal trademarks on 'Triumph', reserving the signature clicks, gasps and diverse other exclamations for solo album tracks. Nonetheless, the fourth Jacksons album for Epic is a good set. It will be the last time one can say that about a Jacksons group record.

They again wrote and produced all of the material and used primarily the same studio musicians, but there is a distinct move away from the "band" sound of *Destiny* into grander arrangements and bigger productions. Five of the nine tracks were issued as the A-sides of singles, so we can assume that neither the record company nor the group were entirely displeased with the album. But its sales were probably squeezed by *Off The Wall*. As far as the group was concerned, this was history repeating itself because the launch of Michael's solo career at Motown had signalled the beginning of the end of the 5's meteoric rise.

Michael as The Scarecrow in *The Wiz, 1979*

CAN YOU FEEL IT

A dramatic, inspirational and uplifting fanfare brings us to attention. Martial drumming sets us in motion. We are the forces of good marching in pursuit of the grail of brotherly love to bring peace and harmony to the world. A disco beat prepares us for attack mode in order to give the 'Men Of War' (see *Destiny)* a final, dire warning that they had better mend their ways before it is too late to save their souls and, indeed, the planet. Musically, the piece, written by Michael and Jackie, builds and shifts emphasis boldly. Timpani, bells, the sweep of strings, the pomp of French horn and cornets combine to bolster the quasi-religious, cosmic message with a big, anthemic, orchestral tone. In these kinds of song it is tempting to hear a measure of the Armaggedon-style teachings of Jehovah's Witnesses, to whom The Jacksons were aligned.

LOVELY ONE

This first single off *Triumph,* written by Michael and Randy, mixes elements of 'Don't Stop 'Til You Get Enough' from *Off The Wall* and 'Shake Your Body' and 'The Things I Do For You' from *Destiny,* which indicates the beginnings of a very stylised approach to recording Michael Jackson dance tracks.

YOUR WAYS

A deliberately eerie sound created the right ambience for a Jackie Jackson song about a relationship with a very strange girl. Michael sings much of it falsetto, a lot of it in a wispy, ghostly style. Odd, effective.

EVERYBODY

Co-written by Michael, Tito and Mike McKinney, 'Everybody' is a free-flowing dance track with chunky horns and prominent bass guitar (McKinney was The Jacksons' road bass player at this time). The song's message – dance your blues away – could not be simpler.

HEARTBREAK HOTEL

Michael's own song and an ambitious production. It is a story of straight revenge as the narrator meets once again a lover he'd left, or stood up, and 10 years on she prepares to take terrible revenge after trapping him in the hotel room in which they should have made their previous rendezvous. Or, as the quiet piano/cello ending suggests, it was all a dreadful dream from which he is just waking, doubtless as the sun breaks through curtains, as is the standard scenario in these cases. All very Hammer horror and easy to see as a dry run for 'Thriller'. The nightmarish wail at the beginning of the track was the recording début of La Toya Jackson. (Some might suggest that her singing has been all downhill from this moment.) 'Heartbreak Hotel' was the second single off the album.

TIME WAITS FOR NO ONE

Written by Randy and Jackie, this was the *fifth*, count 'em, single lifted from *Triumph,* a ballad with a sugary but still touching melody. A deserted lover waits and wonders if his love's coming back this time. There is one great line, about being scared as he wonders if she has someone else sleeping beside her, before the tick-tock of the clock in the lonely room fades the cut.

WALK RIGHT NOW

Nathan Watts' monster bass part sets the tempo for a song, not the last in the Michael Jackson canon, about a girl who just won't accept that the affair is over. She calls, she batters on the door, but, he knows, give in to her and she'll soon do him wrong again. (Imagine him as Michael Douglas and her as Glenn Close.) The track is brimful with interest as the string arrangement follows the bass line and the staccato horns jab into the melody like a knife. Like 'Heartbreak Hotel', this song has a good, well-visualised narrative. It's easy to imagine how it could "play" on stage or, more importantly, video. Michael, Jackie and Randy co-wrote the song, which became the album's fourth single.

GIVE IT UP

A happy, pretty, airy, fly-away kind of a piano-based song, in which all of the group have the opportunity to sing.

WONDERING WHO

A lame song, the worst on the album. Written by Jackie and Randy.

LIVE

Epic EPC 88562
released November, 1981
CD release CDEPC 37545

As live albums go, not one of the greats. As Jacksons albums go, not one of the greats. As Jacksons live albums go, the only one. Interesting because it shows the increasing bias towards Jackson as a solo star. Recorded on the 1981 tour, on which the 'Movie And Rap' portion contained archive film clips. The touring band comprised: Jonathan Moffett (drums), David Williams (guitar), Michael McKinney (bass), Bill Wolfer (keyboards), Wesley Phillips, Cloris Grimes, Alan Prater, Roderick McMorris (the East Coast Horns).

Tracks: 'Can You Feel It', 'Things I Do For You', 'Off The Wall', 'Ben', 'Heartbreak Hotel', 'She's Out Of My Life', 'Movie And Rap' (includes excerpts of 'I Want You Back', 'Never Can Say Goodbye', 'Got To Be There'), Medley: 'I Want You Back', 'ABC', 'The Love You Save', 'I'll Be There', 'Rock With You', 'Lovely One', 'Working Day And Night', 'Don't

Stop 'Til You Get Enough', 'Shake Your Body (Down To The Ground)'.

VICTORY

Epic EPC 86303
Released July, 1984
CD release EPC 450450-2

After the success of *Thriller,* his second Epic solo album, which dominated pop music for most of 1982 and 1983, 1984 should have been a tremendous year of consolidation, relaxation and pursuit of movie projects for Michael Jackson. There was also the prospect of an "official" reunion with brother Jermaine, almost a decade after the split with Motown. In fact, for Michael Jackson 1984 turned out to have much in common with the waking nightmare quality of the George Orwell novel that shares the same name as the year.

First, Jackson's hair was set alight while filming one of the commercials in a multi-million dollar deal struck by him and his brothers to advertise Pepsi Cola. Second, he made this album with his brothers. Third, he was an unwilling participant in a 55-date tour to promote the album, which attracted as much bitter, negative publicity – centring on the price of the tickets, the fact that they were not using African-American promoters and general marketing greed – as he had endured up to that time.

One could see why the album needed the support of a major tour. *Victory* was another misguided attempt at presenting The Jacksons as a genuine democratic creative force and not a group focused on one unique talent. Not only is the songwriting shared out more evenly, the vocals are too. Surely by now the penny must have dropped that none, repeat none, of the other Jacksons have particularly interesting, emotive voices? But no. Michael, keen to pursue his own career with a passion, is reined in to work, unenthusiastically by the sound of it, in the family cause. He contributed only two songs to the album and it is doubtful if either of them would have got past the first selection process for a solo album.

Of course, all spontaneity was fast being drained out of modern American records as overdubs, synthesizer programmes, multi-tracking and diverse other whatnots were used to camouflage the vacuous nature of the music and lyrics. The well-respected Los Angeles studio band Toto guest on several of the tracks. It is a dull, dull album, a Pyrrhic *Victory*.

TORTURE
Indeed. Jermaine, back in the fold, shares lead vocals with Michael on this rocker written by Jackie, who arranged and produced too. Although there is noise of whooshing and whacking and slapping thanks to a synthesizer, this is not as crazed a track as it would like you to think. By no means the worst track on the album, though.

WAIT
An uptempo LA rock song written to Formula 37 by Jackie in cahoots with David Paich of Toto, 'Wait' sounds more like a Toto cut than a Jacksons track. Jackie sings the lead, Michael graces with ad-libs at the very end of the track. It was recorded at four studio locations and required two project co-ordinators. Did someone say it's only rock 'n' roll?

ONE MORE CHANCE
Randy Jackson's attempt to slip into brother Michael's ballad territory but using a couple of Jimmy Jam and Terry Lewis production tricks. Pleasant at best but ultimately ineffectual.

BE NOT ALWAYS

One of the least impressive Michael Jackson songs. At first, the lyric – and there were "additional lyrics" by Marlon – seems like a peculiar exercise in seeing how often the word "always" can be slipped into a lyric without the listener going mad. A strange kind of torture, or parodic joke, perhaps? The words convey a sense of despair at man's inhumanity to man, the suffering, the way the world is heading. As at the end of 'She's Out Of My Life' from *Off The Wall,* he sounds on the verge of tears. He used Bruce Swedien, his engineer from *Off The Wall* and *Thriller,* to work on his two 'Victory' cuts, the second being...

THE HURT

Randy wrote it with David Paich and Steve Porcaro, and with those two men of Toto provided all of the music via keyboards and synthesizers. Unfortunately, Randy sang as well in an unbelievably annoying falsetto. Here was the real hurt.

BODY

Marlon's feature is an extraordinarily silly piece, a "girl I want your body" type lyric set to a melody that would have been rejected during their teeny-bop days. Greg Wright's guitar solo is from better days.

"There are times when I wish I wasn't so recognisable and I could just go out and have a good time. Like being able to go to Disneyland and just go on the rides."

STATE OF SHOCK

Apart from the initials MJ, the Michaels Jackson and Jagger appear to have little in common but it's interesting to hear how the challenge of singing with/against each other on a track gets them reaching. The structure is simple, as is the guitar-based music, and the instrumentation is sparse and metallic – just Jackson's Linn programming and handclaps, David Williams on guitar and bass and Paulinho da Costa on percussion – but bearing in mind some of the overblown yet empty tracks on *Victory* that's no bad thing. "Look at me," the Rolling Stone says in varying murmurous tones at the end of the track, trying to sound like Robert De Niro in a Martin Scorsese movie or Dennis Hopper reading for Quentin Tarantino.

WE CAN CHANGE THE WORLD

Tito's track, written, produced and sung thereby, deeply spiritual and meaningful, entirely forgettable.

THE JACKSONS

2300 JACKSON STREET

Epic EPC 463352
released July, 1989

As if to say "Who needs you?", the next album from the group is The Jacksons *sans* Michael Jackson. (OK, he does a tiny cameo on the title track but so do the children of sister Rebbie and brothers Jackie, Tito, Jermaine and Marlon. Oh, Marlon himself had quit the group by now too, in case you didn't notice.) As a piece of work, *2300*

Michael & Quincy Jones

them. Randy, or Randall as his advancing years now decreed, sang it with the confidence of a man who has found his range and can stay within it.

Two Michael Omartian productions bookend the album. 'Art Of Madness' starts with a misquote from Portia's "the quality of mercy" speech from Shakespeare's *The Merchant Of Venice* and presents an argument that again misquotes the Bard (here there is "art" not method in madness) to beg sympathy for misunderstood genius. The other Omartian contribution, the final track, is a Jermaine-sung ballad titled 'If You'd Only Believe', a nice mid-tempo song about constancy in love and hope for the future.

In similar 'lurve' mood, Jermaine's 'Maria' sounds as though it was conceived as a ballad and when that didn't work they've tried it as a snappy upbeat cut. Erich Bulling's loud drum programming is ultra-prominent. Lee Oskar, a refugee from War, guests on harmonica. Jermaine also sings lead pleasantly on Diane Warren's mid-tempo 'Private Affair'.

Jackie and Jermaine share the lead on 'Alright With Me', a lighter pop confection co-produced by Attala Zane Giles. The group and Giles collaborate on three more tracks – 'Play It Up', 'Harley', a hymn to a piece of machinery in which it's hard to think that they're not playing at being Prince, and 'Midnight Rendezvous', a groove-all-night song set in a somewhat threatening club. Surely bro' Michael would've chosen a venue that was more fun? Cheekily, The Jacksons imitate the gloved one's trademark catch in the voice.

Finally, that title track. It paints a picture of love and harmony chez Jackson in Gary, Indiana. Books by various members of the family have not accorded with this view. It's a nice enough cut, though, and is reprised during a couple of the later tracks.

Jackson Street is more honest than *Triumph*, though it would not be hard to argue that it might just as easily have been released as a Jermaine Jackson solo album. He sings most of the leads and co-writes on all but three of the 11 tracks.

The Jacksons recruited a team of hip producers/writers (notably Teddy Riley and LA Reid & Babyface). With no input from MJ, the swingbeat crispness of LA/Babyface's 'Nothin (That Compares 2 U)', with vocals by Randy and Jermaine, is the best cut. There's more socking swingbeat on 'She', a Teddy Riley/Gene Griffin production from a time when it was debatable whether Riley or Jimmy Jam-Terry Lewis had the funk with

PART IV

MICHAEL JACKSON SOLO: THE EPIC YEARS

The third group album for Epic, *Destiny*, established the appeal and potential of Michael Jackson's writing. While recording it, he'd begun to store away ideas he'd prefer to work on himself rather than with his brothers. Even though he'd been increasingly unhappy, his performances on the tour promoting 'Destiny' cemented his widening appeal. In spite of a lack of confidence about his future, the next logical step was to re-establish the solo career that had been dormant since 1975.

He took some serious business decisions – notably not renewing his management contract with his father when it expired in 1979 but making him co-manager with Freddie DeMann and Ron Weisner of Weisner-DeMann Entertainment, a firm with mainstream clout – and cast around for a producer in order to make his records feel and sound sufficiently different from the group records. According to Jackson in his *Moonwalk* memoir, he called Quincy Jones (the producer with whom he'd built a good rapport during their brief but promising collaboration in cutting 'Ease On Down The Road' and 'You Can't Win' for *The Wiz* soundtrack) to ask for advice in selecting a producer. Those conversations ended with Jones accepting the role. The result of this partnership is well known. With producer Bruce Swedien, a select band of studio musicians and writers such as Rod Temperton, the team broke all sales records and established Jackson as the recording phenomenon of his generation, whose vocal tone and mannerism would be copied as profusely as were Frank Sinatra's, Elvis Presley's or Aretha Franklin's.

The album was originally to be called *Girlfriend* after a song given to Michael by Paul McCartney before the Jones/Jackson project got under way. Assuming that Jackson didn't want the song, the former Beatle recorded 'Girlfriend' for his own *London Town* album. Nothing daunted, Jackson went ahead and recorded it, along with nine other tracks. Two were written by the singer, one by Jackson and Louis Johnson of Brothers Johnson, one by Stevie Wonder and Wonderlove singer Susaye Greene, another by Tom Bahler, another by singer-songwriter Carole Bayer Sager with David Foster, and three by Heatwave's keyboard player and hit writer, Rod Temperton, one of which became the album's new title track. The 10 songs produced five hit singles. Those tracks not used as A-sides in their own right turned up on B-sides, two of them not being required until A-sides off the second Epic solo album needed flips.

Before getting down to work on the first new solo album in four years, Jones and Jackson recut 'You Can't Win' from *The Wiz* soundtrack. Released ahead of the album in April, 1979, it was not a hit and was used as promotional extra, slipped in to some early copies of the impending album. It would be a long, long time before one could again say that a Michael Jackson solo single had failed to chart.

OFF THE WALL

Epic EPC 83468
August, 1979
CD releases – CDEPC 83468,
December, 1983; as a twofer with
Dangerous, 465802 2D, February, 1993

Although A. N. Other album would sell considerably more copies, this is regarded as his best album by many, and certainly by this writer. Four of the tracks were Top 10 hits in the US, it sold 12 million worldwide, it stayed on the UK charts for 173 weeks and in Britain was the first album ever to spawn five hit singles. At this time of dawning massive success in his professional life Michael's personal life was a mess. A shy young man of 21 whose social skills were underdeveloped, he had few genuine friends and was still locked in to his brothers' career by a mixture of duty and guilt.

But no matter what his state of mind or heart, when he came to work he was clearly focused. With Jones, he created a wonderfully well-balanced mixture of fleet-

footed dance tracks, frothy love songs and dreamily romantic interludes, a mixture of pop, disco, soul and light funk that's hard to fault. When I interviewed Rod Temperton about his songwriting techniques he made an interesting comment on the way in which composing had been changed by technology, the market and the way people heard music. "I still feel that I'm really not and never was a songwriter. To qualify that, I really don't think this is the age of the songwriter. When George Gershwin and those kind of people were around, they wrote songs. They wrote on a piano, there was a melody, chords and it stood up on its own. Today, we're writing *records* not songs. You've got to know how to make a record. And so that's what I do. I write to go on tape and the song is never usually finished until the day it goes in the shop."

DON'T STOP 'TIL YOU GET ENOUGH

And here is a song, not written by Temperton but by Jackson alone, that nonetheless amply illustrates his point.

After a quietly spoken intro, above bass and gently shaken maracas, about the Power of the Force that "make me feel like, it make me feel like WHOOO!!" the track is launched by a big, brief horn and swirling string arrangement, which subliminally suggests the grandeur of a movie theme. There is then a sudden distillation into a tightly condensed dance hit. At its heart is David Williams' crisp guitar picking, which gives the constant impression of forward motion. The percussion patrol, led by Paulinho da Costa but augmented by Jackson, his brother Randy and Richard Heath, decorates the track with attractive tinkling and popping, and the rhythm section is all subdued efficiency, there always, but making no fuss about it, just keeping the engine running, wheels turning. Now, it may be that Jackson heard all of this in his head when writing the piece but if that is the case then what he "heard" was closer to architecture than composition. The sounds are built, stacked. This is best illustrated on the fade in which Jones strips away instruments layer by layer until the throbbing centre is revealed, the guitars and percussion, interlocked and acting as one. It's a technique that will be used many times by many others but rarely quite so effectively.

Michael's multi-tracked vocal has a lead part sung almost too high and answered by the lower pitch of his less desperate-sounding second lead. The lyric, about the unseen Force that moves physically and emotionally, can be read as Force = physical passion, Force = spiritual love, Force = the emotional release of dance and doubtless means all three. The first single off the album and released at the same time as the LP, 'Don't Stop' was a No 1 US hit, a No 3 UK hit and, astonishingly, the only Grammy nomination he got that year as Best R&B Vocal Performance, Male and Best Disco Recording. The former it won, the latter it lost to Gloria Gaynor's 'I Will Survive'. (Gaynor also turned The Jackson 5's 'Never Can Say Goodbye' into a disco smash.) It received no nominations for any of the Pop or Rock or Songwriting categories. He would soon exact full revenge for this slight.

ROCK WITH YOU

Originally, when contacted by Quincy Jones to write for his Rufus and Michael Jackson projects, Rod Temperton had insisted that he was too busy. He'd left Heatwave six months earlier but was committed to work on their third album now due. Jones persuaded him to write one song for each artist. Temperton was very keen to work with Jones so he agreed. Because he had not met and got to know Jackson – his preferred way of working – Temperton decided to write more than one song and let the artist and producer choose the one they liked. 'Rock With You' was a rhythm section idea, which under Jones' direction got a softer and more melodic treatment.

The schedule involved Temperton finishing the Heatwave session at 5am on a Saturday morning in New York, flying to Los Angeles and being driven straight to the studios. "I arrived and there was all these top LA session musicians and Q kinda pushes me from behind and says 'Fellas, this is Rod Temperton, hit it. Rod, I'll be in the box'. I guess that was the luckiest thing that ever happened to me because it did have to be some kind of fluke that Quincy and I hit it off that well from first shaking hands. There was always the trust." The three rhythm tracks were cut in two six-hour sessions – 1pm to 7pm on Saturday and Sunday. At the end, Temperton asked which one did they like, was there one they could use? Jones said, 'All three'. He conned me!" Temperton flew back to New York to finish the Heatwave album and write the lyrics for Jackson's three songs. Back on the West Coast he rehearsed the lead melodies with Michael, who learned the lyrics overnight and cut the whole background and lead vocals in one Sunday afternoon. Temperton's three contributions took, in all, about 24 hours of studio time. It certainly launched the songwriter's career into the stratosphere and helped establish Michael's new market.

Drummer John Robinson sets the tempo of 'Rock With You' at a pace that is quicker

than it sounds because the slightly wistful melody gives the piece a slower, swaying feel. The lyrics again draw a parallel between dance and sex. Clipped horn interjections from the Seawind Horns, in one section sounding not unlike a Herb Alpert Tijuana Brass arrangement, and sweeping strings embellish the track's simple heart. 'Rock With You' was the third single off the album, the second US No 1 and reached No 7 in the UK.

GET ON THE FLOOR

Co-written by Jackson and Louis Johnson, the bassist known as "Thunder Thumbs" out of Brothers Johnson. It completed a side of tuneful, unremittingly energetic dance music, not as stiff, stylised or regimented as disco but aimed at the feet as surely as the pair of shiny black patent leather loafers Jackson wore for the album sleeve shot.

"My dancing just comes about spontaneously. Some things I've done for years until people have marked them as my style, but it's all spontaneous reactions. People have named certain dances after me, like the spin I do, but I can't even remember how I started the spin – it just came about."

WORKING DAY AND NIGHT

The second Jackson composition and another punishing dance track. The percussion section – Da Costa, Jackson and Robinson, Michael, also using his voice as a percussive instrument – is in full spate as we walk into the studio. He's soon singing in a style already familiar from *Destiny* with the gasps and catches of breath which he'd now restrict to his own tracks. His multi-tracked background vocals closely mirror what The Jacksons might have sung.

It's the track that is the most "band-like" on the album. Two instrumental breaks feature the rhythm section in cracking form as the guitar emphasises its part, and the horn section spatters an arrangement out of the Earth, Wind & Fire handbook. It's Jackson's band. 'Working' was the flip side when 'Off The Wall' was released as the second single off the album in November, 1979.

Johnson's burbling, bubbling bass and Robinson's four-on-the-floor drumming ground the rhythm track. Melodically, the song is more of a piece with the gliding feel of 'Rock With You'. The horns punctuate Jackson's vocal but it's the strings that pull the track back to the melody from a full-out rhythm section stomp. Jackson's singing is very free now, from the aggressive "chant" to the obvious pleasure he gets from sailing along on top of the groove – at one point he laughs out loud from the sheer pleasure of it all. 'Get On The Floor' appeared on the flip side of 'Rock With You'.

OFF THE WALL

The song Rod Temperton thought Jones and Jackson would select out of the three he'd written. "I tried to find out about Michael's character. I knew he loved Charlie Chaplin and I thought 'Off The Wall' was a nice thing... that was the 'A' song." It continues the theme of dancing away your cares and woe to another great rhythm track that moves at a fast walking pace. His lead vocal is slightly tougher than usual while the creamy background voicings on the chorus are gorgeous. And there are plenty of reference points back to Jackson's songs. The invitation in the chorus to "just enjoy yourself" recalls the group's hit, and the clustered-note emphasis in the last two beats of alternate bars is another Jacksons reference. The odd, eerie voices and manic laughter at the start of the track give a pre-echo of 'Thriller'. But 'Off The Wall' kicks along and stands alone as an optimistic statement about the future, that despite setbacks, life isn't so bad.

GIRLFRIEND
The song written by Paul McCartney for Michael. Essentially, it is the story of a snitch as the narrator tells the girlfriend of the title that he is going to tell her "other" boyfriend about her split affections. The pretty melody, cute performance, jaunty arrangement with Louis Johnson's poppin' bass prominent, create a happy, sunny atmosphere. This camouflages the narrator's intentions, which seem both single-minded and determined and rather sly and underhand. The fifth and final single off the album, it was the least successful and only reached No 41 in the UK. It wasn't released in the US.

SHE'S OUT OF MY LIFE
The outstanding ballad on the album, written by Tom Bahler and best known for the singer's virtual collapse into tears on the final "life". Johnny Mandel's sentimental string arrangement sets up the opening statement by Greg Phillinganes' electric piano and Larry Carlton's crying guitar. The girlfriend has gone and he's aching with helpless, hopeless hurt. To this point, he'd not sung a ballad better. This is the first time his singing about loss sounds like painfully learned experience rather than the imitation of an experience. After three straight dance hits, it was released as the fourth single and went to No 3 in the UK, No 10 in the US.

I CAN'T HELP IT
Even if there were no songwriting credits, we could not mistake this as anything other than a Stevie Wonder song. Co-written with Susaye Greene, the melody, the chord changes, the kick into the chorus, the mood, are entirely El Toro Negro. Greg Phillinganes sprinkles electric piano notes like stardust and his synthesizer warbles phrases that are so obviously in Wonder's style. It's a song about being happily, helplessly in love with lyrics a touch more sensual than Jackson would have written at this time. The track was used on the B-side of 'Don't Stop 'Til You Get Enough'.

IT'S THE FALLING IN LOVE
Carole Bayer Sager had built a reputation as lyricist to Marvin Hamlisch – they co-wrote the Grammy-nominated film tune 'Nobody Does It Better' from the James Bond movie *The Spy Who Loved Me*. David Foster was a writer, arranger, producer and musician with a burgeoning reputation who had written for R&B groups such as Earth, Wind & Fire. Not obvious collaborators, perhaps, but this has lyrics such as you'd hear sung to a romantic comedy film tune, a quite heady, bubbly atmosphere. To précis the storyline, falling in love makes you happy, being in love makes you sad. Anyone over the age of, what, 14, 15 can relate to this. Sung as a duet with session singer Patti Austin (she sings the opening refrain), the song springs to life each time they snap into the effervescent, beaty choruses. Listen, too, to Louis Johnson's nimble bass playing. The cut was used as the B-side of 'Billie Jean'.

BURN THIS DISCO OUT
The final Temperton tune closes the album on a stomping theme and lyrics tailored to Jackson's passion for, and ease with, dance. The lyrics are little more than a series of linked, and clichéd, words and phrases descriptive of a good time on the dancefloor – "groove", "boogie", "beat", "spin the sounds", "raise the roof", "get on down" – and a final fine time is

offered by the band, Louis Johnson nailing the bass but good. Marlo Henderson, late of Wonderlove, and David Williams keep up a chatter of guitars and blasting Seawind horns in their best Earth, Wind & Fire mode. The track was used as the flip to 'Beat It'.

THRILLER

Epic EPC85930
December, 1982
CD release CDEPC 85930
December, 1983

After the success of *Off The Wall,* artistic as much as commercial, Jackson became something of a session animal. Short of erecting flashing neon lights that read "These Pipes For Hire" he could not have got more in the way of background vocal business. Projects included individual tracks on albums (all released in 1980-82) by Stevie Wonder, Diana Ross, Brothers Johnson, Quincy Jones, Donna Summer, Minnie Riperton, sister La Toya Jackson, Kenny Loggins (late of Loggins & Messina), Dave Mason (late of Traffic), crossover country star Kenny Rogers, songwriter Carole Bayer Sager and Joe "King" Carrasco. On the Ross album *Silk Electric* he wrote and produced 'Muscles'; on La Toya's eponymous effort for Polydor, he produced and co-wrote 'Night Time Lover'.

In between this action he was coerced into recording another Jacksons set, *Triumph,* which saw a marked diminution in his contribution, outstripped only by the diminution of his nose. Yes, even before

Off The Wall, the sustained teasing by his brothers and father had finally fattened the cosmetic surgeons' wallets. Michael's profile changed in other ways. With the increased sales of his albums came increased media attention and the desire for titbits of "inside" information with which to titillate readers, listeners and viewers. His media profile was raised. Here was an area over which he could exercise little control. He was not comfortable with interviews, did not give great quotes, and so throughout the Eighties the media focused on the cloistered lifestyle, the menagerie and a burgeoning reputation of Michael as Genuine Oddball.

What hurt even more than the cosmetic surgeon's scalpel was the rejection by the National Academy of Recording Arts And Sciences in nominating 'Don't Stop 'Til You Get Enough' for only two Grammies, awarding it one and ignoring 'Off The Wall' entirely. Rewards and awards were important to Michael. Moreover, it was clear that the album was one of the biggest sellers of the year and was also a tastemaker. By any criteria, it was a winner. To top it, Jackson and Jones reassembled substantially the

Michael & Quincy at The Grammys, 1983

same crew, but as well as guests with jazz, soul or (Stevie) Wonderlove chops – Larry Carlton, George Duke, Phil Upchurch, Wah Wah Watson, Marlo Henderson – they also hired rock-orientated players in order to give the music a less subtle sound and feel. The set's original title, *Starlight,* seems singularly inappropriate.

Again, he wrote a good proportion of the material – four of the nine tracks – with three more from Rod Temperton, including another title track that tapped straight into the singer's fascination with movies. However, the alteration in Michael's writing was the critical factor. It was as though he'd been in therapy to teach him how to express anger. All of the songs he wrote are about conflict, although one of them is clearly light-hearted in intention.

serious business in an industry suffering a recession. In fact, the album's success in pulling buyers into the record stores was helping the sales of other acts.

When the dust finally settled, Michael Jackson's second Epic solo album had sold a staggering 51 million copies. And he got his Grammies. At the Awards ceremony, actor Mickey Rooney, one of the presenters, said early on, "It's a pleasure doing The Michael Jackson Show" as the singer collected Album of the Year, Record of the Year (for 'Beat It'), Best Pop Vocal Performance, Male, Best Rock Vocal Performance, Male (for 'Beat It'), Best New Rhythm & Blues Song and Best R&B Vocal Performance, Male (both for 'Billie Jean') and Best Recording For Children (for narration and vocals on *E.T. The Extra-*

"[My sisters] never wanted to be in the group. Besides, if we let Janet in the group she'd have eaten up all the profits."

The result, *Thriller,* provoked a sort of vinyl, tape and CD feeding frenzy the like of which had not been seen since the emergence of The Beatles, when singles were still the stock-in-trade of the pop music industry, and certainly has not been equalled since. (In 1964, The Beatles had 11 Top 10 hits in the US; in 1983, when singles were mostly important adjuncts to album sales, Michael had seven Top 10 hits.) Sales were boosted by several marketing coups.

As noted, seven of the nine tracks were hit singles, each one hoovering up more album sales. Videos with high production values were shot to promote the singles and Michael eventually broke through MTV's racial barrier. After three hit singles, his appearance on the *Motown 25: Yesterday, Today, Forever* NBC-TV special – the Moonwalk dance was seen by an estimated 47 million viewers – gave the album yet another boost. By June, 1983 it had sold 10 million copies worldwide, over seven million of them in the US. This was

Terrestrial based on the Steven Speilberg movie, which made him cry even more than 'She's Out Of My Life'). *Thriller* engineer Bruce Swedien won the Grammy for Best Engineered Recording (Non-Classical) and Quincy Jones and Jackson picked up Producer Of The Year (Non-Classical). In the US, the TV audience for the Awards was 60 million. In the week following the broadcast, *Thriller* sold another million copies in the US alone.

 WANNA BE STARTIN' SOMETHIN'

Written by Michael at the time *Off The Wall* was being recorded, there are obvious rhythmic parallels with 'Don't Stop 'Til You Get Enough' in the busy percussion section and David Williams' guitar. But there's a shift towards synthesizers (Greg Phillinganes and Bill Wolfer) as carriers of the rhythm. The real change is in the tenor of the lyrics – there is anger at gossips' vicious tongues, at treachery and cunning

of false friends – and he hurls insults ("you're a vegetable") and introduces Billie Jean, always talking, a motor-mouth, "tellin' lies and rubbish". He offers practical and moral advice too – if you can't afford to look after and raise a child, don't get pregnant, otherwise you'll find yourself stealing or the baby "slowly dyin". But he ends on a hopeful note – look to your personal pride, believe in yourself – buoyed up by a joyful African chant. The track was the fourth single, released in June, 1983, backed with The Jacksons' 'Rock With You', a No 8 UK hit and No 5 US hit.

BABY BE MINE

The first of the three Temperton songs opens with a drum fill closely reprising the start to 'Rock With You' and grooves merrily into a mid-tempo love song of irrepressibly sunny disposition. In spite of the presence of a small regiment of synthesizer players/programmers (six of them, actually), drummer Ndugu Chancler keeps the track grounded giving it a pop-swing, particularly in the bubbly choruses. Oddly, it appeared only as a B-side to 'I Just Can't Stop Loving You'.

THE GIRL IS MINE

After the success of 'Girlfriend', the song Paul McCartney wrote for Jackson, a rematch was perhaps inevitable. At the time, McCartney's career was not at its perkiest and the critics were, as ever, condemning him for not being John Lennon. So Jackson's invitation to duet on this pleasant stroll through an AOR melody offered a welcome return to very familiar territory. Although Jackson wrote it, 'The Girl Is Mine' sounds like the sort of song McCartney writes in his sleep. This is credit, again, to Jackson's aforementioned "sponge"-like quality, the way he can absorb people's styles. (Subsequently, Jackson and McCartney worked together on 'Say Say Say' and 'The Man', both of which appeared on McCartney's *Pipes Of Peace* album.) Although it is supposedly an argument between two friends over a girl's affections, she might not be flattered by the mild, jokey tones adopted here, which suggest that at the end of the day no woman is going to come between their friendship.

Far from the strongest track on the album, it was the first to be released as a single. "We really didn't have much choice," Jackson explained in *Moonwalk*. A duet between McCartney and Jackson would be playlisted unto oblivion and perish through over-exposure soon after the album came out. "We had to get it out of the way" by releasing it up front as a single. Not an outstanding advertisement for the album, it nonetheless reached No 8 in the UK and was a No 2 US hit. It's middle of the road winsomeness is similar to McCartney's collaborations with Stevie Wonder on 'Ebony & Ivory'.

A few years later, while McCartney was visiting Jackson's LA home, Michael asked him how best to invest the massive fortune *Thriller* had earned. "In song publishing," replied the former Beatle who had lately acquired most of Buddy Holly's song catalogue. Michael took Paul's advice to heart and promptly bought ATV, Music which owned Northern Songs, the Lennon/McCartney Beatle catalogue. They have not recorded together since.

THRILLER

There obviously comes a time when trying to find something new to say about a work that has sold over 50 million copies seems just a little fatuous. This is that time. Does anyone *not* know about this track? Has anyone in the radiocentric world *not* heard it? Or 'Billie Jean' or 'Beat It'? Written by Rod Temperton as a homage to horror movies, 'Thriller' creaks open with a door that could use some oil, echoing footsteps, a howling wolf and a howling wind. The dance groove, rolling in like fog on the moors, resolves into an evenly paced 4/4, driven solely by synthesizers and only David Williams' guitar hinting at funky syncopation. Jackson again sings with a harder edge – as he'd done on 'Wanna Be Startin' Somethin'' – but the crowning glory is the fruity closing recitation, or "rap" as it is inappropriately named on the sleeve, using the resonant, haunted tones of the late, great Vincent Price, who put the ham in Hammer Studios' horror movies. Laughably,

Jackson felt moved to treat seriously the accusations that 'Thriller' implied approval of occult practices and to issue an official denial. This, too, may have helped to shift more copies. The fifth single off the album, it was a No 10 UK hit.

BEAT IT

Michael gets pragmatic and kicks down the doors of MTV by cutting a straight, lumpen 4/4 rock track laced with an unbelievably fussy and flashy rock guitar solo courtesy of Eddie Van Halen. It clearly belongs on a different track but, hey, if it gets exposure on MTV, who's to care? Steve Lukather and Paul Jackson add further rock guitar riffing. Lyrically, we find Michael in his *alter ego* guise as Ice-J. He cuts the macho pull of the gang's colours but stresses the advisability of getting out before the kid becomes just another statistic. It was released as a single while its predecessor, 'Billie Jean', was still climbing the charts and ensured an almost complete takeover of the airwaves. It was a No 3 UK hit, No 1 US.

BILLIE JEAN

At one point this song was to be re-titled 'Not My Lover' because Jones thought listeners might confuse the object of writer Jackson's ire with Billie Jean King, the tennis player. A celebrity of Jackson's stature is, as a matter of course it seems, plagued by a number of damaged or deluded people who think they have some claim on or against him. (And some may even be right.) The character filing a paternity suit in 'Billie Jean' is a composite of these lost souls, he admitted in *Moonwalk*.

Sung in an aching, angry voice with the full range of gasps, squeals and catches, the lyric is delivered in the style of one giving evidence under cross examination, the passion of the story and the plea of innocence increasing from the plaintive to the bitterly declamatory as the track progresses. Dean Parks' terse guitar solo manages to say a lot with a few notes through the sheer bite of his playing. 'Billie Jean' was a No 1 in both the US and UK.

HUMAN NATURE

After the anger and aggression of 'Beat It' and 'Billie Jean', the mollifying effects of a sensual mid-tempo pop ballad are not to be sneered at and this delightful tune by John Bettis and Steve Porcaro exactly fits the bill. Porcaro's Toto lay down a billowy, pillowy wash of LA studio sounds and Jackson's voice at its most breathy and feverish as city streets call him to their night life. And if you think that the song, ostensibly about the joys of singles dating, sounds strangely at odds with the preceding track you are not alone. Lovely sound though.

P.Y.T (PRETTY YOUNG THING)

'Human Nature' ends with Jackson waking up, touching "her" shoulder, hearing the call of the street again. Almost immediately he's in the next track, huskily whispering how good she makes him feel so let's be off into the city night. Subliminal connections like this are what's expected from a canny producer like Jones. 'P.Y.T' is a sharp little dancer, co-written by James Ingram, one of the best singers in Jones' circle, and Quincy himself. Satisfactory enough in its pop-soul way, there is less to it than at first meets the ear. Cute and quite catchy, its attraction is its fizzy drive, courtesy of Ndugu Chancler's drums, but aside from the oft-repeated 'P.Y.T.' hook of the title, melodically there is not much to linger in the memory. The dance market was enough to turn it into a No 11 UK hit.

THE LADY IN MY LIFE

The final track is a Rod Temperton ballad and A Very Interesting One at that. It is one of the few occasions on which Jackson tries to take on the mantle of 'Lurve Man' à la Teddy Pendergrass. This is not apparent during the first two verses and choruses and one only gets a hint of it in the bridge. But after Paul Jackson's chords lay out and Louis Johnson starts poppin' his bass guitar, we suddenly find ourselves in the presence of Jackson, shirt open to the navel, extrapolating in increasingly urgent fashion about what he's going to give "his lady" and whereabouts he's going to give it to her (i.e. "all over"). Hey! He done growed up.

BAD

Epic EPC 450290-2
September, 1987

In art, sport, business, science, in any field of endeavour it is natural, even desirable, that one should want to improve on past performance. Michael Jackson was as driven in this respect as anyone. Conflicting public utterances during the two years it took to make suggested that at times Jackson felt he must produce a record that sold more than *Thriller.* Other times, he must just do the best he could. And there was the rub. An artist's "best" work is not always that which sells the most copies, be it a book, record or any mass-produced article. In pop music, so many other factors come in to play – the state of the market, prevailing trends and fashion, what other "product" is available at the time, all-round appeal of the artist or group, the clout wielded by the act and his, her or their record label, management company and other associates.

Almost all factors were in Michael's favour when *Thriller* followed the superior *Off The Wall* and outsold it fourfold. In *Moonwalk*, Michael describes the initial reaction of "outsiders" to *Thriller* as, well, less than thrilled. He went away and finished a new song, remixed some of the rest and – "presto!" – everyone was delighted. And so now he had to prove himself all over again.

Sheryl Crow on stage with Michael

There must have been a certain fear at facing the public again. If the new record doesn't sell over 51 million copies, someone's going to cry "Failure!" even if it is the biggest-selling album of the year. In the meantime there had been the utter

stories out of half-truths and pure fiction – tabloid journalists make a very good living at displaying such ingenuity – and so the snapshot of Wacko Jacko was developed. So, a few members of the Jehovah's Witnesses proclaim him as the new Messiah,

"Certain people were created for certain things, and I think our job is to entertain the world. I don't see no other thing that I could be doing."

fiasco of the Victory tour in 1984, which did far more to sell *Thriller* than The Jacksons' *Victory,* and the steady trickle of stories about his offstage and record life. Through these the media gradually constructed a picture of a terminally wacky Peter Pan-like creature with more money than he knew what to do with who could also make some fairly bold and hard business moves, such as buying up the ATV publishing catalogue, which included all of the best Lennon & McCartney Beatles songs, for a cool $47.5m. If there is no hard news to print it is easy to improvise big

he is waxworked at Madame Tussauds, he records 'We Are The World' in aid of African famine relief, he tries to buy the bones of John Merrick, the Elephant Man, he films *Captain Eo* for Disney, he devises a plan to live until he's 150, he launches a range of stuffed, fluffy animals – Michael's Pets – and does more sessions and /or production for Diana Ross, Rockwell, Jennifer Holliday, Jermaine, Janet and Rebbie Jackson and Stevie Wonder. And he took two-and-a-half years to write and record *Bad.*

In the four years between *Thriller* and *Bad* pop music had moved on. The sound of African-American music got harder, partly through the use of studio and new instrument technology, and also thanks to tougher lyrics and subject matter as rap, hip-hop and swingbeat gave 'streetsier' voice to new generations. But to record the 1987 follow-up he'd assembled the usual suspects – producer Jones, engineer Swedien, synthesizer maestro Phillinganes, a smattering of Toto – plus guest duettists Stevie Wonder (replacing McCartney, miffed at the ATV deal) and Siedah Garrett, a young girl singer "discovered" by Jones, and musicians such as jazz organist Jimmy Smith and rock guitarist Steve Stevens, from Billy Idol's band.

"The Thrill Is Back!!" promised the sticker on *Bad,* '10 Brand New Hits!!!' Even allowing for the most generous interpretation of the word "hits", this was some way wide of the mark. Jackson wrote eight of the 10 songs and, in a desperate search for a hard, contemporary sound, the rhythm arrangements leaned too heavily on the dink-donk-dunk of synthesizers. Who is going to tell a young man whose previous record sold over 50 million copies that he has made some wrong choices? The arrangements forced Jackson to sing in a more aggressive tone, which was not always convincing, and, after the first two tracks, too many of the songs were too soon forgotten. That said, there is a messianic tone to many of the lyrics. Now that all of those souls have responded to his music perhaps he can lead them to a better understanding, to brotherly love, to tolerant human values. After wearing a tuxedo for the cover shot of *Off The Wall* and a white suit for *Thriller,* the black jacket, belted, buckled and zippered in every spare inch, looked preposterous. The change in facial bone structure and lightening skin tone (which he blames on a vegetarian diet) has been even more radical.

Such was the barrage of pre-release hype about the follow-up to the biggest-selling album ever worldwide, that the initial sales in the first week of availability were impressive – 350,000 in five days in Britain, where one in four albums sold in that period were *Bad* – and it was not without longevity, staying in the US Top 5 for 38 weeks. The brouhaha also sparked renewed sales of *Off The Wall* and *Thriller.* He also promoted the album with a world tour and multi-million dollar budgeted videos. It had four consecutive No 1s pulled off it – only the soundtrack to *Saturday Night Fever* had achieved that before – and Jackson became the first artist to have four consecutive No 1s as a group member and as a solo artist. In its first nine months, *Bad* sold 15 million copies worldwide.

BAD

'Wanna Be Startin' Somethin' opened *Thriller* with a challenge and *Bad* does the same. The macho showdown – he's returning to his 'hood a wiser, worldlier man – is resolved by Jackson's assertion that the world can be a better place but he still invites a fight if they think he's wrong. He's "bad" as in "baaad". A strong start musically, too, with the solid, unsyncopated thud of 4/4 and a chorus catching hold whether the listener likes it or not. Released as the second single off the album in September, 1987, it reached No 3 in the UK, No 1 in the US.

THE WAY YOU MAKE ME FEEL

Love makes him feel pretty good, in fact, on one of the album's more cheerful songs with his multi-tracked background voices echoing his lines in the catchy, if predictable, chorus and the bompin' synthesizers and sockin' drums keeping the rhythm on the case. The third single, also reached No 3 in the UK, and, in the US, his third consecutive No 1 from the album.

SPEED DEMON

Whether Michael had been to one drag race meeting too many or seen one road movie too many, the requirements of singing a song about the dangers of speed do not sit well with his voice. His attempts to sing hard and mechanical make his voice sound constrained, there is no freedom, merely the restriction of a straitjacket.

LIBERIAN GIRL

A song that doesn't quite work. At one point titled 'Pyramid Girl', the locale was changed from north east Africa to west, and the African dialect used is Swahili, from South Africa. Some confusion here. The melody isn't as memorable as the apparent charms of the young woman being serenaded. It was the final single lifted off the album, in July 1989, and reached No 13 in the UK.

JUST GOOD FRIENDS

The song, more suited to duet partner Stevie Wonder than to Jackson, was written by Terry Britten and Graham Lyle, UK writers who had not long before penned big hits for Tina Turner. Jackson and Wonder discuss which of them is truly loved by the girl in the middle – shades of 'The Girl Is Mine' – and although the chorus has some attraction the production is driven by an annoyingly uneven drum sound. 'Friends' is a track that should work well, indeed almost does so, but fails to properly resolve the parts into a satisfactory whole. Jackson returned the favour by duetting 'Get It' on Wonder's 1988 album *Characters*.

ANOTHER PART OF ME

A clarion call to human brotherhood sung against banks of impersonal synthesizers and drum programmes. Sometimes, the contrast between warm flesh and cold metal works well. Here, the twain never meet. The song was used in the *Captain Eo* movie and was the sixth single and peaking at No 15 in the UK, and No 11 in the US.

MAN IN THE MIRROR

One of the successes of the album because of the sheer power of the assembled gospel voices – The Andrae

Crouch choir, the Winans family group – letting rip in sanctified, sumptuous unison. Written by Siedah Garrett and Glenn Ballard, the lyric advises anyone wishing to change the world, or a part of it, to look in the mirror and start the reassessment with the person you see there. This notion of taking charge of one's own destiny and responsibilities for the wider common good is boosted by an uplifting melody and, most importantly, by a choir charged up with evangelical electricity. And there is some truth in the idea that if you're not happy with yourself, there's a good chance you won't be happy with anyone else. Fourth single, peaked at No 21 in the UK and, in the US, the fourth consecutive No 1 off the album.

I JUST CAN'T STOP LOVING YOU

The Jackson-penned duet. After Barbra Streisand and Whitney Houston turned down the invitation to sing on it, Qwest staffer Siedah Garrett was brought in. Opening with whispered pillow talk, the

ballad evolves into an unexceptional boy-girl exchange of 'true-lurve' vows. The first single, again like *Thriller,* which kicked off with 'The Girl Is Mine', it was released in July, 1987 and, remarkably, made No 1 in the UK.

DIRTY DIANA

The album's 'Beat It', an attempt at hard rock, with Steve Stevens' quasi heavy metal guitar as the instrumental icing. The subject is a woman willing to sleep her way to a recording contract. Michael may have met several and heard about many others. 'Dirty Diana' was the fifth single, No 4 in the UK and, inevitably, No 1 in the US.

SMOOTH CRIMINAL

Again an attempt to replicate a successful track from the previous album. The cinematic theme of 'Thriller' is here replaced by a woman-in-peril scenario, very Hitchcockian (the inner sleeve shows a silhouette of Jackson and engineer Swedien in profile, the latter portly in the manner of the great director). The video shot for the track cost $8m, equivalent to the budget for a tight independent feature-length movie shoot. 'Smooth Criminal' was the album's seventh single, reaching No 8 in the UK and No 7 in the US.

LEAVE ME ALONE

A bonus track on the CD. Layers of vocals give a rich, airy texture to a song that carries a blunt, personal message from the singer. The plea for a level of privacy is heartfelt and tinged with the feelings of hunted paranoia and persecution that inhabit much of his writing in the Epic years. The song's title is to be taken entirely literally. He spends much of the next year accepting awards, attending premières and other photo opportunities and doing many well-publicised charitable deeds. 'Leave Me Alone' was released as a single in the UK where it peaked at No 2. It was not a single in the US.

DANGEROUS

Epic EPC 465802-2
November, 1991
released as twofer with Off The Wall
on 465802 2D, February, 1993

Jackson had spent as much time on the record-breaking world tour to promote *Bad* as he'd spent recording it. Didn't sell as many copies as *Thriller* but it was the biggest-selling album of 1987 and continued to sell through the next 12 months. By the end of the Eighties he'd sold 110m records in the decade. But the incessant barrage of publicity and hype – and the indisputable fact that *Off The Wall* and *Thriller* were better records – created a swell of anti-Jackson feeling, given particularly loud voice in the English-speaking white rock press. The host of Jacko Is Wacko type stories that were regularly regurgitated by the tabloid press, despite denials and explanations, created a clear picture that Michael Jackson was synonymous with odd behaviour. Tabloid newspapers never let the truth spoil a good story but, that said, Jackson is plainly not like you or me. (Do readers believe tabloid stories? In 1989, readers of tabloid newspapers tended to vote high for Jackson in popularity polls; the more "cerebral" publications rated him low.)

As the selling of *Bad* wound down, the tour was announced as Michael's last world trek. The slim memoir, *Moonwalk,* was published and movie *Moonwalker* released. (It's soon on video and outsells *The Making Of Thriller*.)

He split, after four years, with manager Frank Dileo. He began to record tracks for his fourth Epic solo album at the end of 1989 and after a year its release was put back to the early summer of 1991, then to late summer and finally to November. He worked on an estimated 70 songs before paring them down to 14. By then he'd signed a new records and films deal with Sony, who'd bought Epic's parent Columbia, which could earn up to a billion dollars. The contract was announced as lasting 15 years requiring six albums and giving an immediate $18m advance for the first new music project. His royalty on each album was 25 per cent.

After three albums with Quincy Jones, Jackson broke the tie and hired Teddy Riley, the writer/producer who'd virtually defined the new swingbeat with Guy, his own trio, and with productions for young, hip acts. If Jackson wanted to get back to "blacker" sounds, he'd made an intelligent choice. Half of the 14 new songs on *Dangerous* were co-written and/or produced with Riley. Jackson produced the rest with engineer Bruce Swedien or with another co-writer, Bill Bottrell, and the results spread over a double album or single CD. The guests used on the tracks – rapper Heavy D, metal guitarist Slash from Guns N'Roses – gave

Jackson's masked eyes peer through an ornate Mark Ryden illustration, populated by elephants, a crowned dog and bird, each in regal finery (sceptre and orb included), other birds (a peacock included of course), animals and insects, young children, cherubim and seraphim, Greek statuary, a fairground ride that disappears into a post-*Metropolis* industrial maze and produces healthy children but skeletal animals. The detail, which is easier to see on the vinyl rather than CD or cassette sleeve, signifies the subject matter of the tracks.

The world tour in support of the album again sparked sales of all of his previous solo albums. In Britain, all four were in the Top 50 albums as was a Special Tour Souvenir Pack, a four-picture CD box set with the tracks 'Off The Wall', 'She's Out Of My Life', 'Don't Stop 'Til You Get Enough', 'Thriller', 'Beat It', 'Billie Jean', 'Bad', 'Dirty Diana', 'Smooth Criminal', 'Dangerous', 'Remember The Time', 'Black Or White'. In the US, sales of *Dangerous* had been sluggish (by his standards) until he engineered appearances on two of the highest profile TV shows – singing four songs as the half-time entertainment to the 1993 Super Bowl (133million viewers) and chatting on *The Oprah Winfrey Show* (85million).

> **"I could never go solo, not with the group being a family thing because it would be like breaking away from my family. Anyway, the other guys are doing some solo things too and we're still recording as a group."**

a fair warning to expect a greater exaggeration of the split between hard-edged, modern, synthesized dance sounds and "rock" songs on the one hand and softer, more traditional ballads on the other.

A word about the album sleeve. After three portraits culminating in the buckled-up and zipped-down punk/biker look of *Bad*, *Dangerous* has a more obtuse cover.

JAM
Breaking glass comes before the breaks. Riley sets out assertive, punctuating blasts on synthesizer over the top of the tight, 4/4 dance beat. The lyric is an unfocused ramble through current issues: help your neighbour, live each day as though it's your last, don't surf religions, be happy within yourself. All of which suggests that the

woodeny 4/4 beat, but the cut-the-crap admission of bone-on-bone lust is a product more readily associated with a certain Minneapolis recording studio than the Neverland Ranch. Again, there is much breaking glass. The single, number three off the album, reached No 6 in the US, No 8 in the UK. (By now, of course, it takes very few sales to get a record into the lower reaches of the singles charts. They had lost importance, for established artists, as anything other than an album marketing tool.)

SHE DRIVES ME WILD

Car revs up, horn honks, the 4/4 beat is loud and locked. Against it, Jackson sings the verses tough and the choruses tender. And, it has to be said, the way he swoons over the look of the girl, the feel of the track owes as much to Prince as anyone.

REMEMBER THE TIME

A swingbeat remembrance of past love that starts off reminiscing sweetly about long romantic phone calls but by the fade is urgently priapic in recalling assignations in the park, at the beach, in Spain. Clearly, this man has some emotion to work through and is probably not yet finished with the relationship. The second single off the album reached No 3 in both the US and UK.

CAN'T LET HER GET AWAY

Another strong-armed synthesized swingbeat 4/4 and more male obsessiveness as Michael desperately clings to a woman who seems hell-bent on breaking off the affair.

HEAL THE WORLD

The first track on *Dangerous not* co-produced by Teddy Riley marking the Scene two Act one of the album. Written alone by Jackson, 'Heal The World' is a pantheist plea for global love and harmony to save the world for future generations. He sings it in a warm, relaxed tone and makes the most of the melody's several

bottom line is: each of us is on our own. Heavy D raps briefly, says Michael J is def. One of his least successful singles, it reached No 26 in the US and No 13 in the UK.

WHY YOU WANNA TRIP ON ME

Or why pay so much attention to MJ when a huge proportion of the world doesn't have enough to eat and there are problems in schools, on the street, people have no homes, fatal diseases are epidemic, there is widespread corruption and on and on. Jackson sings the verses in a reined-in, frustrated style and the choruses in a freer, fuller-throated fashion to give freer expression to his annoyance. The door slams. It's over. Paul Jackson Jr's loud and angry guitar introduction and the feel of the rhythm has an echo of Prince's work.

IN THE CLOSET

Speaking of Prince, there is a large step towards (hetero)sexual revelation between consenting partners here. Whispered endearments reminiscent of the pillow talk on 'I Just Can't Stop Loving You' don't prepare the listener for the sparse,

Michael filming the *Black Or White* video

hooks, gliding easily over the anthemic arrangement. This is deeply influenced by movie themes, improving choral works and uplifting music used in the advertising of international branded names, which is what the Heal The World Foundation became. A No 27 US hit and No 2 UK hit.

 ### BLACK OR WHITE
Humour had not formed a major part of Jackson's *oeuvre* yet the overture to this track, which comes at the midway point of *Dangerous,* has the chime of recognition as a father batters on his son's bedroom door demanding that he turn off the loud rock (guitarist Slash of Guns N'Roses obliging). An exchange of views on the "do it!"/"won't!" level ensues. Imagine a row from any Roseanne Barr TV show. The kid gets antsy and he changes tape muttering "Eat this" and 'Black Or White' plays. Polemical in content and delivery, the song's anti-racist message could not be more straightforward. He's not scared of "sheets" (i.e. the Ku Klux Klan) and refuses to live defined as "a colour". The video

screened to promote this track, which was the first single off the album (No 1 in both the UK and US, which made him the first act to have a No 1 hit in the Seventies, Eighties and Nineties), and caused considerable moral outcry because of its images of Jackson on the rampage, shattering windows and rubbing his crotch.

 ### WHO IS IT
Written solely by Jackson, another angry song in which a sense of wider betrayal burns through the superficial storyline of a man left lonely by a woman. He uses the trademark catches and gasps in his voice too often and there is an over-familiarity about the chorus, but the juxtaposition of his pent-up fury singing against his sweeter, multi-tracked background vocals works extremely well. He sang this a capella on the *Oprah Winfrey Show* and public demand resulted in its release as a single. A No 10 UK hit, and No 14 US hit.

GIVE IN TO ME

Well, here's sound evidence, if you really wanted it, that he could sing lead in a heavy metal band. We do not need Slash's guitar solo to tell us that this is a rock ballad because the clichéd images of passion and the hackneyed rhymes – "desi-yah", "fi-yah", "hi-yah" – are warning enough. Eminently forgettable.

WILL YOU BE THERE

Having dipped his toe in the turgid pool of heavy metal he plunges headlong into inspirational gospel. A choral arrangement lifted from a performance of Beethoven's 9th Symphony by the Cleveland Orchestra opens this BIG track (and resulted in a $7m lawsuit against Jackson, his MJJ Productions company and Epic – which Sony settled out of court). Later copies of the album CD credit Ludwig van B's part in the track. Again, the tune and arrangement have familiar progressions but his voicing against the full might of the Crouch Choir is unexpectedly passionate. A gospel album might have great artistic rewards. He ends the track with a spoken prayer, which will have considerable resonance during the next few years. Two "special" versions of the song appeared on the soundtrack to *Free Willy*, a movie about a boy and his friend, the Killer Whale.

KEEP THE FAITH

Co-written with Jackson by Siedah Garrett and Glenn Ballard, it's less of a churchy success than 'Will You Be There' or 'Man In The Mirror', which Garrett/Ballard penned for *Bad*. The song, which is not strong on melody, gets good, as they say, only after roughly four-and-a-half minutes when Jackson starts spitting out lyrics and the Crouch Choir gets fully involved.

GONE TOO SOON

A Larry Grossman/Buz Kohan ballad. He might have recorded this at the time of *Ben*.

DANGEROUS

After much industrial banging and clanking, like the soundtrack to David Lynch's early movies (*Eraserhead, The Elephant Man*), we are back in the land of Teddy Riley's swingbeat for one last time. A relentless off-beat drives the track, there is not much melody to speak of and the lyric centres on woman as predator, again.

HISTORY: Past, Present And Future Book 1

Epic EPC 474709-2
June, 1995

In August 1993, the roof fell in on Jackson, metaphorically, when the singer was accused of child abuse: object, 13-year-old Jordy Schwarz Chandler. Throughout the Eighties and early Nineties, Jackson had given freely and generously to sick and underprivileged children and built up an image of one who treated all children with largesse. So this was an utterly devastating charge. He cancelled concerts and later claimed to have become dependent on painkillers to get him through the world tour. A videotaped interview revealed a narcotised Jackson looking blurry and slurring words. Most business associates continued to support him but Pepsi-Cola severed its links.

Early in the investigation, the Los Angeles police suggested that Evan Chandler, Jordy's father, had tried and failed to get Jackson's backing for a film project, and carried out his threat to "expose" the singer as a child molester. This story ran and ran. Until January 1994, in fact, when the LA police admitted they'd too little evidence to charge Chandler *père* with extortion, that the evidence against Jackson was poor (descriptions by the boy of Jackson's genitalia did not match the photographic evidence obtained by the police) and the Chandler vs Jackson case was settled for an undisclosed sum. Innocent until proven guilty, Jackson never had his day in court to refute the charges.

Against this difficult, oppressive and sordid background, in which many parties were manifestly on the make, the saga of *HISTORY* also ran. A 'Greatest Hits' album had been planned as early as 1989. This one was originally scheduled for November 1993 release as a 'Greatest Hits' album with two or three bonus tracks, but the project was delayed by (a) slow production of the new songs, (b) continuing uncertainty about the outcome of child abuse accusations and concomitant negative publicity, (c) a subsequent desire to match the 'Hits' CD with a CD of new music and (d) marriage to Lisa Marie Presley, only daughter of Elvis.

And lo, after the slings and arrows of outrageous accusation and a hostile 10-year media campaign, he shall arise anew, born as a phoenix from the ashes of a burnt-out career. Or, in fact, he shall appear as a huge statue, Stalinesque in its massiveness, hauled on a barge up the River Thames in London and elsewhere. Jackson's music on *HISTORY* is often very angry. True, the lyrics and spat-out singing style had been gestating since the *Bad* LP but the indignation and sense of frustration is palpable. To salve this simmering rage, he had only to leaf through the 52-page booklet and read the messages of support therein from Elizabeth Taylor, Steven Spielberg and the late Jackie Onassis (reprinted from the *Moonwalk* foreword) or glow over the list of awards, stretching over four tightly packed pages and accumulated over 14 tightly packed years, gaze at photographs with four Presidents of the United States of America

and with Nelson Mandela, or pore over his own messages of thanks to friends, to helpers, to the dear departed and to the children of the world, which go on for four pages. It is all terribly uplifting.

CD-1 *HISTORY* BEGINS: 'Billie Jean', 'The Way You Make Me Feel', 'Black Or White', 'Rock With You', 'She's Out Of My Life', 'Bad', 'I Just Can't Stop Loving You', 'Man In The Mirror', 'Thriller', 'Beat It', 'The Girl Is Mine', 'Remember The Time', 'Don't Stop 'Til You Get Enough', 'Wanna Be Startin' Somethin'', 'Heal The World'.

CD-2 *HISTORY* CONTINUES:

SCREAM

The first (new) single off the CD, a duet with Janet, was written and produced by Jimmy Jam and Terry Lewis, graduates of the Minneapolis school of funk whose studio work had turned Janet Jackson into a worldwide star. Opens with fuzzed, pharty notes and tones, screams, shattering glass and clattering noise. The lyric mentions injustice, lies, game-playing, rule-breaking, confusion, mercy, pressure, disgust. (The illustration in the booklet depicts a cornered child, dressed only in underclothes, screaming. This suggests, loudly, that the lyric is not about the recent campaign of accusation, persecution, harassment and extortion to which Jackson felt he had been subjected but about abused children.)

THEY DON'T CARE ABOUT US

By using three simple sentences spoken by three streetwise kids above a children's choir as the intro to this angriest of angry tracks, Jackson invokes both the innocence and the knowing instincts of children to understand his part of the modern world. "Them" not caring about

of the late Seventies and early Eighties and complements a simple lyric of emotional displacement, loneliness and "outsideness".

THIS TIME AROUND

Someone wants to get him good, use and falsely accuse him, sings Jackson. Autobiography? Nooooo. The bassbastic, mid-tempo, sledgehammer rhythm banging like a headache that a person who felt persecuted might get, matches another pent-up vocal. The real world breaks in on Jackson's personalised grievances as the Notorious B.I.G. raps on the intrusions of life as lived at a (slightly) less public level with flashing cameras, phone taps, break-ins and on and on.

"In a crowd I'm afraid. On stage I'm safe. I'd sleep on stage if I could. See, my whole life has been on stage and the impression I get of people is applause, standing ovations and running after you."

"us" is at least as old as Greek democracy or the pharaohs, but Jackson is concerned only with Franklin D Roosevelt and Martin Luther King, who would not have been silent in the face of continuing, growing injustices in American society. The tap dance of synthesized 4/4 rhythm makes a stark, energetic backdrop to his tirade against racism, persecution, police brutality, the stripping away of rights. The ugly, angry rock guitar is, for once, entirely appropriate to Jackson's mix. Of course, the general points are meant to be specific to his recent past. Even the pursuit of the tabloids during the previous 10 years had not prepared him for the events of 1994. He'd been given a jolt into political and social understanding. It is also about the death of the American dream. Recent autobiography? Nooooooo.

STRANGER IN MOSCOW

After the bile of the first two tracks, comes cleansing rain. A lovely melody that harks back to his best ballads

EARTH SONG

BIG anthem with a melody Elton John might have written. The humanitarian and ecological bill so far is enumerated: the destruction of people, flora, fauna, yea the very planet itself. In the final third the Andrae Crouch Singers step up to the microphone, Jackson's voice slips into "angry" mode, the volume and arrangement are cranked up and the agenda is repeated in a monumental, quasi-Baptist finale.

D.S.

Back on solid ground, Jackson again confronts the demons from his recent past by creating a one-dimensional character from the far right. In another clench-throated, rock-arranged rant, "Dom Sheldon" is a persecutor who rubs shoulders with the CIA, communicates with the FBI and, Jackson wonders, hunkers down with the Klan. Such are his enemies.

MONEY

Who needs it? Certainly not Jackson. If he could take it with him he would never need to work again in his next 20 lives. One hopes he has a firm grasp of the power given to the 'owner' by great sums of money. In "Money" he is very clear about what other people – individuals, the state, religions – will do to get a share of it. What they will do is – anything.

COME TOGETHER

Since leaving Motown, Jackson had almost never done a cover version. This remake of The Beatles' last hit was an idea he'd been kicking around for some years. He attacks the off-beat and verses harder than had the Fabs and fights an honourable draw with the choruses.
He doesn't add much to the song, and the song doesn't reveal anything we didn't already know about him.

YOU ARE NOT ALONE

Written by bare-chested balladeer R. Kelly and nicely sung by Jackson in a simple, warm, straightforward style that would have fitted into any of his late Seventies and early Eighties albums (solo or with The Jacksons).

CHILDHOOD
(THEME FROM WILLY 2)

Sequel to the killer whale movie (he'd recorded 'Will You Be There' for the first one) gets a whopping production just waiting for Streisand, Ross or Houston and a lyric storyline that may seem strangely familiar. Jackson laments a lost childhood, that's why he likes "elemental things", so before judging him, remember he had been denied the chance to grow up ordinarily. Michael, folks have bought over 50 million copies of *Thriller,* one is tempted to observe, and very few people on this earth are wealthier than you. In this respect, global society has repaid its debt.

TABLOID JUNKIE

But in this respect, the debate rages on. Starting with, and continually interrupted by, a recitation of the "weirdo" stories about "Wacko", this is as much a condemnation of the people who read, believe and repeat the stories in what used to be called the "yellow" and "gutter" press as those who invent, write and publish them. As any good advertising executive or propagandist will know, repetition is the currency of perceived rather than actual truth. Unfortunately, the track is a lot less interesting than its subject matter.

2 BAD

In purely arrangers' terms, this is Jackson's funkiest track – as James Brown, George Clinton and Sly Stone might understand the feel. Guys rap, there is a quote from 'King Of Rock' and the keyboard funk riff rolls tough like an Isley Brothers track. In these circumstances, the clichéd lyrics really don't matter a damn. Basketball star Shaquille O'Neal raps.

HISTORY

This ambitious, complicated concept track deserves more careful unstitching and decoding than it received from critics on its release. It breaks down into four parts, which recur at intervals throughout the closely interwoven composition. It's certainly unlikely that any pop track ever crammed in as much reference-book material as '*His*tory'.
'Part one' has a myriad quotes, musical and spoken. These range from the opening sample, borrowed from the final, monumental 'Great Gate Of Kiev' movement of Modeste Mussorgky's blessed 'Pictures At An Exhibition' to American marching bands. (His use of Russian classical music chimes with the influence of celebratory Soviet statuary as the image on the album illustration. The original is in Volvograd but it's got a different face, hair and "uniform".) From newsreel snippets featuring the announcement of Charles Lindbergh's solo flight across the Atlantic, to Muhammad Ali and the young Queen Elizabeth II, from Martin Luther King to Thomas Edison reciting 'Mary Had A Little Lamb' on one of the first phonographs, Edward Kennedy's eulogy at

the memorial service for his assassinated elder brother Robert, and, finally, the Apollo astronauts words from the Moon.

This babble of news items closes the track. Parts two, three and four, which shove each other aside like argumentative verses, are music-and-lyric based. The second theme is akin to an angry 'Come Together', the sound of the rage that drives aggressors to invade and defenders to fight their corner and bring redemption. The hard-edged message is: don't let people put you down, move on up. The third segment begs eternal questions about human suffering. Like, how many victims and struggles must there be before freedom and fairness become fact? When will man listen to "the prophets' plan"? (Point of order: many of the "fights" are about which prophet is right.) The scan of the lyrics here recalls 'Blowin' In The Wind' but the logic of the lyrics, which are compassionate, is less than precise. The section segues easily three times into part four, the part that provides answers – the broad thrust of which are that every conquest will end in liberty. As a world view it relies on the wildly optimistic hope that we are creating the best of all possible worlds, that the 20th century's heroics and many, many genocides are all part of the long journey to world harmony. This final part gets an uplifting, full-blast pseudo rock-gospel treatment.

LITTLE SUSIE

Trying to make "art", much less "pop music", out of the story of the death of a child is fraught with dangers – starting at ultra-sentimentality moving quickly through to sheer bad taste. In overall effect, Jackson's attempt is Dickensian rather than, say, operatic. A choral choir sings Duruflé's 'Pie Jesus' requiem, a child hums affectingly to the gentle melody of a music box. We are primed for tears. Then, a song in which a child falls downstairs and dies. The investigation, as the crowd gathers, reveals a sad life – father left home, mother died, the child is neglected. The arrangement, highly strung, realises the song in a very

cinematic fashion and creates an emotion not unlike an overwrought "Eleanor Rigby". At the end, the bell tolls sombrely. It's a difficult and, one imagines, heartfelt subject.

SMILE

The CD's opening tracks were bristling with anger and indignation and the closing tracks become increasingly maudlin and sombre. So Jackson uses the melody, written by one of his heroes, Charlie Chaplin, and sings it like a Broadway trouper to end the 15 tracks on a wistful, hopeful, tuneful note. Heartache, sadness, sorrow, tears, fear, will all disappear if you just smile. (NB: Not really folks, but after a diet of unassuaged anger you'll be needing something light and optimistic to help you face the world without a weapon in your hand.)

INVINCIBLE

Epic EPC495174 2
October, 2001

After many delays Michael's first solo album of new material for six years was finally released amid of barrage of publicity, not all of it welcome. In the years between *HISTORY* and *Invincible* his personal life and general well-being had come under considerable scrutiny, not least because his appearance had changed dramatically from the cute little African-American boy who fronted the J5. Michael's hair was now straight, his nose sharply pointed and, most remarkably, his skin appeared to be getting

and theme park, complete with fairground rides. His best friend was a chimpanzee named Bubbles.

Invincible cost a reported $30m (£21m) to make and involved the efforts of 27 co-writers and seven producers, and it was made available in four different colours: red, blue, green and gold. The sleeve featured a simple, unadorned shot of Michael's face. Among the contributors were Notorious B.I.G., R Kelly, Teddy Riley, Timbaland and Rodney Jerkins contributing to the overall sound. The guitarist Carlos Santana made a memorable contribution on one track too.

Jerkins later talked about how on occasions he and Michael worked into the early hours of the morning on the album. "We slept in the Sony studios in New York for two weeks straight on couches, and we didn't go to no hotel, no apartments, no nothing. We just slept on couches and worked," he said. "It gets kinda smelly at times, but that's what

lighter. He had married a second time, to Debbie Rowe, a nurse who produced his two children, a boy, Prince Michael, and a girl, Paris, before they separated. A third child, Prince Michael II, was born to a surrogate mother, identity unknown.

"I feel that the world we live in is really a big, huge monumental symphonic orchestra. I believe that in its primordial form, all of creation is sound and that it's not just random sound, that it's music. You've heard the expression 'the music of the spheres'? Well, that's a very literal phrase."

As if all this wasn't enough Michael's behaviour became increasingly erratic as the nineties progressed. He was rarely seen in public without a face mask and was reputed to sleep in a specially built oxygen chamber designed to prolong his life. Minders who surrounded him invariably carried umbrellas to protect him from sunlight. He lived on a ranch near Los Angeles called Neverland, named after the mythical kingdom in J. M. Barrie's fantasy *Peter Pan*, where children never grow up. He had his own private zoo

it's about. That's how you get that fever, that feeling of heat that makes you want to create more because you're not leaving the studio. So instead of you working from 10 to eight and then stopping and going home sleeping, we may wake up at three in the morning and say, 'Let's do a part'."

Not surprisingly, in view of the way Michael's life was careering out of control, there was a reference to this turmoil in a song entitled 'Privacy', which is about media intrusion.

Michael with his chimp 'Bubbles' and a female fan

"Stories are twisted and turned," he sings. "Stop maliciously attacking my integrity."

Many critics complained that the album was too long, and at 16 tracks they had a point, but when it works – as with 'You Rock My World', the only significant hit single, and 'Whatever Happens'- it was an accomplished record even if it lacked songs as memorable as those on *Off The Wall* and *Thriller*. There was an undue emphasis on ballads, with 'The Lost Children' taking a gold medal for sentimentality. At the other end of the spectrum, 'Whatever Happens', in which Jackson tells the tale of a couple involved in some unidentified but threatening situation, is a fine piece of work set to a Latin feel as might be expected with Santana on guitar.

Reviews were mixed, with *All Music* commenting: "Ultimately, the record runs too long, losing steam halfway through…[It's] not enough to make *Invincible* the comeback Jackson needed… but it does offer a reminder that he can really craft good pop." *Rolling Stone* gave the album three stars out

of five, adding that the early R&B tracks were good, but the later ballads made the record too long. "Make no mistake, a good half of *Invincible* rocks bells," wrote *NME*'s reviewer. "But at 76 minutes and 16 tracks the studio clearly never rang with the dreaded words 'no, Michael'."

By November sales were reported to have topped three million worldwide, but despite these promising initial sales, and the fact 'You Rock My World was an international hit, in the long run *Invincible* failed to match the success of Michael's earlier solo work. Total sakles peaked at around 10 million, and sales in Europe and other parts of the world far cxceeded sales in the USA.

Tracks: 1. Unbreakable, 2. Heartbreaker, 3. Invincible, 4. Break Of Dawn, 5. Heaven Can Wait, 6. You Rock My World, 7. Butterflies, 8. Speechless, 9. 2000 Watts, 10. You Are My Life, 11. Privacy, 12. Don't Walk Away, 13. Cry, 14. Lost Children, 15. Whatever Happens, 16. Threatened.

PART V
THE OTHER BROTHERS – AND SISTERS

OTHER JACKSONS AT MOTOWN

With Michael Jackson's solo career successfully launched, it was inevitable – strategically planned, in fact – that the four other brothers would be promoted as solo artists, thereby generating six sources of income. In the event, however, only one was a success. Marlon, a dance track fan, would not record as a solo act until long after the split with Motown. There were plans for an instrumentally-biased album by guitarist Tito. *Jackie Jackson,* a sugary-toned, soft-focus album was released in the US in October, 1973, and January, 1974, in the UK on STML 11249. Michael aside, the only Jackson to record consistently and achieve commercial success was Jermaine, the heart-throb of the group.

Considering his first album, *Jermaine,* released in January, 1973, hit the shops just a month after Michael's *Ben,* it sold well helped by 'Daddy's Home', the follow-up single to 'That's How Love Goes'. 'Daddy's Home', a remake of a 1961 hit by Shep & The Limelites, was a No 9 US pop hit for Jermaine that reached No 3 on the US R&B chart. The low-key comforting ballad was a perfect vehicle for Jermaine's voice, which lacked the exuberant expressiveness of his younger brother's or, indeed, its higher octane emotional fuel. The first single, co-written by producer Johnny Bristol, was a sparkier uptempo song.

Jermaine's next album was two years down the line, *My Name Is Jermaine* coming in October, 1976. By then, he was the only Jackson brother left at Motown, having married Hazel Gordy, Berry's daughter, on December 15, 1974, and stayed put with pa-in-law when the group carried out its intention, first made public on June 30, 1975, to leave the label in search of greater creative freedom. The very title of this first post-split album recognises the need to establish a new identity for himself. *My Name* is a fairly apprehensive start as he works through influences and tries to find his own voice in the post-5 era. It is hard to

"I was raised on stage and I am more comfortable out there than I am right now [being interviewed]. When it comes time to get off, I don't want to. I feel like there are angels protecting me."

Jermaine's second album, *Come Into My Life,* was released in September, 1973, in the UK, two months after Michael's *Music And Me.* It had a greater preponderance of slow songs because, as he readily admitted, they were his forté and he felt and sounded most comfortable with them. Mostly, the tracks were produced by the teams who were working on The Jackson 5 albums: Hal Davis, Fonce Mizell and Freddie Perren, The Corporation, Mel Larson and Jerry Marcellino and the like. A version of Phil Medley's 'A Million To One' is notable. It was produced by Pam Sawyer and Gloria Jones – women producing anyone other than themselves was still extremely rare in the Seventies. 'You're In Good Hands' was an R&B hit in the US in October, 1973, and although he had favoured 'I Need You Now More Than Ever' there was no more pop chart entry. *Come Into My Life* also included a version of 'Ma', the song Norman Whitfield wrote for The Temptations, and 'Sitting On The Edge Of My Mind', "far out, man" being the only fair comment.

underestimate the trauma he felt because of the split. In that respect, the faults of *My Name* can be understood, although that does not make poor tracks such as 'Faithful', 'Who's That Lady' (not The Isley Brothers song) and 'Look Past My Life' any the more palatable. 'Lovely, You're The One' was his favourite track, quite a pretty tune with a mellifluous trombone prominent, and 'Bass Odyssey', produced by Greg Wright, was an instrumental romp showing off Jermaine's chops on the instrument he'd played in the 5. The single 'Let's Be Young Tonight' was a Philly-influenced dance track and made the R&B charts in September, 1976.

The next album, *Feel The Fire,* released in September, 1977, marked further progress with the singer co-writing three of the nine tracks with his co-producer Michael McGloiry and writing one, 'Got To Get You Girl', alone. It actually harked back to The Jackson 5, as though he were getting something out of his system. The title track has an ersatz "live" feel to go with the up-front guitar solo and it, like the ballad 'You Need To Be Loved', was co-written with McGloiry. That last-named song was similar to 'I Wanna Be Closer', a song he'd written for Switch, who were another "family" group (the DeBarges) he'd discovered and taken to Motown. McGloiry's 'Take Time' had pop potential and 'Strong Love', co-written by Greg Wright and Syreeta, was a happy Stevie Wonder-ish sound. 'Git Up And Dance', the third Jackson-McGloiry collaboration, went down to the disco carrying with it a strong hint of Larry Graham, Sly Stone's bassist and leader of Graham Central Station.

The same team worked on four of the nine tracks on *Frontiers,* released in April, 1978. 'Let It Ride', driven by wet funk bass, and the fast, tight 'The Force', which kicked on with the power of a disco group like, say, The Trammps, found Jermaine more confident in his handling of uptempo songs. 'Je Vous Aime Beaucoup', which he co-wrote with Maureen Bailey, had a Smokey Robinson feel, but the sci-fi rip of 'Take A Trip To My Tomorrow (Let's Encounter For The First Time)' was rather too obvious to be a success. Sandra Crouch's 'I Love Every Little Thing About You' was a noisy, lively, rolling, rumbling track, but the remake of Stevie Wonder's 'Isn't She Lovely' had nothing to add to the original and McGloiry's 'Castles Of Sand' might have been better served by The Impressions, Miracles or Temptations.

By far his most successful solo album of this period, artistically and commercially, was the April, 1980, release *Let's Get Serious,* with three of the seven tracks co-produced by Jackson and Stevie Wonder, who also played keyboards, guitar, drums and synthesizer. The title track, written by Wonder and Lee Garrett, is Jermaine's most appealing and enduring solo cut. Big brass, strong bass and a typically arresting Wonder melody. The two other Jackson/Wonder productions are on 'Where Are You Now' and 'You're Supposed To Keep Your Love For Me', which was recorded first (rearranged somewhat in the manner of 'Outside My Window' on *A Journey Through The Secret Life Of Plants,* Stevie's

Janet Jackson

then new album) and persuaded Wonder to do the other two. As with the previous cover 'Isn't She Lovely', Jermaine doesn't exactly wrest ownership of the song from his working partner although 'You're Supposed' creates an irrepressibly sunny mood. The four other tracks had been recorded roughly two years earlier. Two of them were co-written by Jermaine with his wife, Hazel, and Maureen Bailey. 'We Can Put It Back Together' was a wimpish ballad but hidden beneath the superficial story of the break-up of a marriage was, the singer claimed, a heartfelt wish that he and his brothers would be reunited as a group. The song made him weep, he said, and it may indeed bring tears to your eyes. 'Feelin' Free', the second collaboration, set his soft voice against a jerky pop-funk track. Of the rest, 'Burnin' Hot' gets momentum from a driving lead guitar line and 'You Got To Hurry Girl' borrows from Bernard Edwards' bass guitar part on Chic's 'Le Freak'. It's also noticeable that Jermaine's voice had changed – it actually took on a softer-edged quality, which in part he put down to having his tonsils removed.

The success of *Serious* was quickly followed by another solo album simply named *Jermaine,* which came out at the end of 1980. Nine tracks, seven produced by

Jermaine Jackson

Jermaine, who did most of the arranging, singing and background vocalising and wrote or co-wrote all but two of the tracks. The first side is predominantly uptempo, rather more experimental in nature and is dominated by the artist himself. The second side is more predictable and it was hard to find a good reason for the inclusion of the two songs in which he had no hand, 'I Miss You So' and 'Can I Change My Mind' by name. Other talking points: Jermaine at this time started to mention getting back with his brothers for selected projects; on the album's sleeve he is pictured in jodhpurs and with riding crop. He had become enamoured of equestrianism and went horse-back riding with Mr & Mrs Barry White and, one suspects, some extremely strong-backed steeds. White had been very supportive of Jackson when the brothers split from Motown.

The jodhpur motif was continued on 'I Like Your Style', this time in leathers. By the time he began work on the October, 1981, offering, he had formed his own J L Productions company. Jermaine wrote or co-wrote all of the 10 songs except for a version of Wonder's 'Signed, Sealed, Delivered I'm Yours'. Elliot Willensky, composer of 'Got To Be There', collaborated on 'I'm My Brother's Keeper', a title pregnant with meaning. His own 'It's Still Undone' also spoke of unfinished business. 'I'm Just Too Shy' was a reference to his personality; 'Paradise In Your Eyes' the track for romantics. His productions, by now, are assured.

Jermaine's final Motown album, *Let Me Tickle Your Fancy* (August, 1982, the same year as *Thriller)* was co-produced by Jackson and Berry Gordy and all but one of the 10 songs had input from the singer.

Jermaine had always expressed a strong preference for ballads and softer sounds and on his later albums even the dance tracks are performed soft focus. Rhythm arrangement and production values on several tracks, the title cut included, are influenced by the lighter side of Prince and Jimmy Jam/Terry Lewis funk from Minneapolis, Stevie Wonder's vocal style occasionally influences and both sides finish with a ballad. The final song on the album, co-written with Elliot Willensky, shares the same title as the previous album. Jermaine's confidence is apparent in the spread of instruments he plays – keyboards, synthesizer, bass, bass synthesizer, drums and percussion – and the likelihood of a reunited Jackson 6 was increased by the guest appearances by Tito and Randy, the brother who had replaced him in the family act. Some time later, Jermaine decided that his future lay elsewhere. He claimed that there were people at Motown, not Berry Gordy, with whom he could no longer work. In 1983 he quit Motown and signed to Arista. See later section for a rundown on his work for them.

OTHER JACKONS AFTER MOTOWN

This part begs a question that has been at the nub of the family's local difficulties since the early Seventies. Apart from providing Michael with stage decoration, what use were the other members of The Jackson 5? Eldest brother Jackie always had a generational problem – he looked like the sensible Big Brother sent along to keep an eye on the kids. Tito was said to be a good guitarist. On stage, squealing teeny-bop voices drowned out much of what he did because when he did it Michael and/or Jermaine, the heart-throbs, were often dancing. On record, the very occasional features hardly made anyone sit up. Marlon was even less evident. Through good looks and a pleasant if wholly unexceptional voice, Jermaine built a significant following and, as noted in an earlier chapter, built a strong

teeny-bop following. Randy, his replacement, exuded tremendous confidence and energy. As the one who joined the act full-time after their best times at Motown, he always had something to prove.

Among the "other brothers", Jermaine continued to have the highest profile. Even so, in the inevitable round of interviews to publicise each new solo album, his interlocutors were as much interested in his views on, and titbits about, Michael as they were in Jermaine's new album. This always grated, as it did on all of the Jackson siblings. Here is the most telling Jermaine Jackson pronouncement ever on the subject: "I do find it distressing that everybody wants to focus on Michael. Even though Michael is very talented, a lot of his success has been due to timing – and a little luck. It could just as easily have been me." One does hope those words were put into his mouth by a mischievous reporter. There was nothing anyone could do about the fact that Michael had the talent.

Jermaine split with Motown and signed to Arista in 1983, announced he'd be getting back together with his brothers and had an immediate hit album, *Dynamite*. The first single, 'Sweetest Sweetest', was a happy self-produced pop-soul side boosted by backing vocals from Whitney Houston, not yet a star in need of a bodyguard, and rock guitar from Paul Jackson, which set up the catchy choruses. The album's title track was a tighter uptempo dancer and a big US hit, but the standout tracks were 'Tell Me I'm Not Dreamin' (Too Good To Be True)', a duet with Michael, and 'Take Good Care Of My Heart', ditto with Whitney Houston. (The track also appeared on Houston's first solo album as did another duet with JJ, 'Nobody Love Me Like You Do'. The album, Houston's that is, not *Dynamite,* sold 15 million.) Arista had hoped to release 'Dreamin'' as a single but Epic refused clearance on Michael's vocal for fear of harming the sales of *Thriller* and its singles. "This would probably be my only number one ever but I can't put it out," an understandably grumpy Jermaine said.

(The track, minus Michael's voice, was used as the flip of 'Dynamite'.) There was also a reunion with The Jacksons on the singularly ill-advised 'Escape From The Planet Of The Ant Men', a staggeringly dreadful track that did not bode well for the imminent Jacksons *Victory* album and tour. Of the rest, 'Come To Me (One Way Or Another)' was Jermaine's only solo composition on the album, a neat, simple dance track; 'Oh Mother', co-written by the singer and Elliot Willensky of 'Got To Be There' fame, was a Mother's Day card set to sentimental music. (For the record, at this time Jermaine had also duetted with Pia Zadora, an "actress/singer", on something called 'When The Rain Begins To Fall' and had a very nice time filming a big budget video, directed by Bob Giraldi, in Rome.)

The main feature of *Precious Moments* (1986), Jermaine's next album, was an attempt to recapture the success of 'Let's Get Serious', the collaboration with Stevie Wonder that marked his best work at Motown. Lightning did not strike in the same

place twice. 'I Think It's Love', the cut with Wonder, made no bells ring, and there was another duet with Whitney on 'If I Say Your Eyes Are Beautiful'. The year also saw Jackson make his first solo tour since quitting The Jacksons 10 years previously.

By the late Eighties, sister Janet Jackson had become a major star in her own right with Jimmy Jam & Terry Lewis' feisty mix of light funk and pop, and duet partner Whitney Houston had become a major success for Arista. Label boss Clive Davis proudly eyed Houston's achievements in bucking the dance floor and making a career out of big, booming ballads that spoke to the white audience and to middle-class African-Americans. Jermaine was coming off The Jacksons' resoundingly unsuccessful *2300 Jackson Street* so what did he know? Jermaine knuckled down and did as Davis advised. Thus we find his next work of importance, *Don't Take It Personal* (1989), aimed directly at the Whitney Houston market. The title track was written by the group Surface and recorded while Jackson waited, in vain, for New Jack Swing king Teddy Riley to find time for JJ in his schedule. Jermaine also co-wrote 'Two Ships' with Surface, recorded a couple of MOR cuts with Kashif ('Climb Out', 'I'd Like To Get To Know You'). He'd recorded tracks with Larry Blackmon and Cameo but, plainly, if they were in a style anything like Cameo's leering, late-Eighties music they would not sit well in Arista's market view.

Two years on, Jermaine was hitched to hot producers Antonio "LA" Reid and Kenneth 'Babyface' Edmonds. He co-write five of the 11 tracks on *You Said* (1991), including the first single 'You Said, You Said'. As careful planning would have it, Michael's 'Black Or White', the first track off *Dangerous,* was due out at the beginning of November and during the first weekend of that month radio stations also started playing 'Word To The

Jermaine Jackson

"I can't perform if I don't have that kind of ping-pong with the crowd. You know, that kind of cause and effect action, reaction. Because I play off them. They're really feeding me and I'm just acting from their energy."

Badd!!'. The song on the finished album was essentially about a lovers' quarrel. But before Jermaine rewrote the lyrics, they had directly and unambiguously addressed Michael in a not entirely complimentary fashion, suggesting he was a lonely soul, had reconstructed himself and had changed his colour. It included an invitation to Michael to pick up the phone, call Jermaine and talk things over. One can only imagine what he said after the pirate version was aired, giving the tabloid enemy a weapons dump of ammunition.

And whither the Jackson Four – Jackie, Tito, Marlon and Randy?

Marlon, arguably the most artistically self-effacing of all the Jackson brothers, left the group towards the end of the Eighties (he was not on *2300 Jackson Street)* and released an album, *Baby Tonight* (Capitol, 1987). He'd always wanted to do one, he said, even at Motown. "I don't want to be 50 years old and say I wish I'd tried it." He wrote and produced it by himself and played many of the instruments too with the help of Greg Phillinganes. Here was someone who had been putting his leisure time to useful effect. With a bias towards dance and light funk, *Baby Tonight* was a surprise simply because Marlon had been the closest to an "invisible" Jackson.

Randy, who had been a frequent co-writer with Michael on The Jacksons' albums, signed as a solo act to A&M. Jackie, well, he had the good sense to get a knee injury and miss some of the Victory tour.
He divorced from Enid and in 1987 signed as a solo artist to PolyGram.

Tito, meanwhile, was preparing his big project, 3T, better known as Tariano Adaryll, Taryll Arden and Tito Joe Jackson, his three sons. First heard on the soundtrack to *Free Willy* singing 'Didn't Mean To Hurt You', a self-composed mid-tempo ballad sung in voguish teeny-pop nasal style (as opposed to the more traditional, full-throated, diaphragm-heaving style). Assigned soon after to Michael's label, MJJ, co-managed by Tito and Frank Dileo, the trio added 'What Will It Take' to *Free Willy 2* and named their début album *Brotherhood* (1995). Tracks included 'Why', produced by Michael and written by Kenneth "Babyface" Edmonds, and 'Anything', the first single.

Tito Jackson

SISTERS DOIN' IT FOR THEMSELVES

Only the youngest Jackson progeny, Janet (b Janet Damita Jo, 16 August, 1966), has come close to matching Michael's commercial appeal. Not a great singer, as anyone who has heard her indifferent ability with a ballad in "live" circumstances will acknowledge, she's built a career on well-produced records, songs with good hooks and feisty lyrics that catch a mood of self-confidence in life and love, and well-choreographed routines on stage. There's promise of an acting career too including roles in long-running US shows (*Good Times, Diff'rent Strokes, Fame*) and a lead role in John Singleton's movie *Poetic Justice*.

Like her elder sisters, Janet made her first major appearance with the family act at the MGM Grand Theater in Las Vegas in 1974. As the mathematicians among you will agree, she was eight at the time. She went on to work on the family's 1976 CBS TV series, *The Jacksons*. The Sisters twice worked as a trio – once during the running of the series and later in 1981, a project that foundered on the eternal question of post-Supremes trios, who gets to play Diana and who's gonna be Flo and Mary? A year later, Janet signed to A&M. The first side of *Janet Jackson* (UK release February, 1983) was written by Rene & Angela (Rene Moore and Angela Winbush, who later married Ronnie Isley), produced by them with Bobby Watson (of Rufus, some of whom he hauled in as session players) and included the two singles 'Young Love' and 'Say You Do'. Foster Sylvers of The Sylvers, a post-Jackson 5 teenage soul group, and Jerry Weaver produced side two. Janet did not have a big voice to carry the songs; the songs did her voice's limited power and range no favours. Interestingly, according to the credits *none* of the Jackson family contributed so much as a background "hmmmm" or a handclap.

Brother Marlon rectified that on 1984's *Dream Street* (A&M), producing and co-writing two of the nine tracks, Jackie, Tito and Michael adding vocals. European disco producers Giorgio Moroder and Pete Bellotte, who made Donna Summer a disco star, produced five tracks including 'Two To The Power Of Love', a duet with Cliff Richard, which must have meant a lot to the US market. But perhaps the most significant link was Jesse Johnson, former member of the Minneapolis band The Time, who wrote and produced 'Fast Girls' and 'Pretty Boy'.

Janet, encouraged by A&M A&R veep John McClain, decided on her own direction, against the advice of her father. In 1984-86, Joe Jackson was having enough problems trying to keep a finger in Michael's pie, as it were, to concentrate hard on the thus far none-too-promising singing career of his youngest. She took McClain's advice, went to Minneapolis and hitched up with Jimmy Jam and Terry Lewis and their Flyte Tyme production team. In the early and mid-Eighties, Jam-Lewis were a hot team, pumping out hits by Alexander O'Neal and the SOS Band, among others. The 10 tracks they fashioned for Jackson's next album formed a blueprint for her solo career to date. Her spoken introduction to *Control* (1986) – very cool, self-assured and, well, controlled – set out her agenda. When one thinks about it, control is what this big family had always been about. Father controlling sons, Motown controlling sons, sons battling for control of their own lives. Soundwise, pitching Janet in with Jam-Lewis was a masterstroke because they produced a sound utterly unlike Quincy Jones'. Other Jackson solo recordings were in the LA/New York pop-soul mainstream and begged comparison with Michael. *Control* was de-Jacksonised.

The tracks, crafted in the tuneful, tightly funked Minneapolis mainstream in its post-Prince pomp, slipped easily on to radio and the dance floor. Jam-Lewis, and fellow former Timesters Jellybean Johnson and Monte Moir, wrote simply and to Janet's vocal strengths. What she lacked in power she compensated for by a blend of tones – cute and vulnerable but hiding wilfulness and

determination. The lyrics were assertive and designed to keep boyfriends on their toes ('Nasty', 'What Have You Done For Me Lately', in 'He Doesn't Know I'm Alive' she actually debates taking responsibility for catching her man) or sexy and designed to keep boyfriends on their backs, such as 'When I Think Of You'. 'Let's Wait Awhile' keeps him in a state of panting expectation and 'Funny How Time Flies (When You're Having Fun)' is a slow screw that might never have gotten past the patriarch. Hey, she even speaks French and fakes orgasm. *Control* sold 10 million, spinning off six Top 50 hits: 'What Have You Done For Me Lately' and 'Let's Wait Awhile' (both No 3), 'When I Think Of You' (No 10), 'Nasty' (No 19), 'The Pleasure Principle' (No 24) and 'Control' (No 49) and an epidemic of remixes.

The follow-up took three years to record and release in which time she also started and scrapped an album titled *Scandal* and re-negotiated her A&M deal. The one-nation world manifesto of *Janet Jackson's Rhythm Nation 1814* (1989) shared many of the anti-racist, socio-political concerns evident in some of brother Michael's songs but focused much more sharply on them through lyrics and inserts between tracks, which spelt them out in a very unambiguous way. Like him, she can focus on problems (as in 'State Of The World') but offers no solutions – to be fair, she was only 22 and must have observed much of this from behind the Encino barricades. Also, on the cover, videos and tour, she showed a Michaelean taste for dressing up in a military uniform, her 'Rhythm Nation' outfit being a utilitarian version. The first three tracks set the manifesto. Did we get the point, she asks? "Good," she adds, "now let's dance". And, indeed, the rest is almost entirely given over to a good dance record, although the ballad 'Livin' In A World (They Didn't Make)' echoes her brother's suffer the little children thoughts. The album sold eight million, spawned seven hits and a monster world tour that rejuvenated the doubts about her voice as an instrument of strength and emotion, which Jam-Lewis had so cleverly camouflaged in the Flyte Tyme studio. Ballads, as ever, gave her away.

Her obligations to A&M satisfied, she signed to Virgin for $32m in 1991 and began paying back her advance in 1993 with *janet.* coming, like the seven singles lifted from it, in a profusion of packages and remixes with sparkly bits, lumpy things and other "immediate collectors' item" gewgaws added on. The subject of this marketing blitzkrieg was another collaboration with Jam-Lewis but with more guests, from Public Enemy rapper Chuck D to opera singer Kathleen Battle. *janet.* is a better set than *Rhythm Nation* but not as solid a joy as the effervescent *Control,* which has better melodies. We have slow sex ('That's The Way Love Goes', 'The Body That Loves You'), fast sex ('Throb') and impulsive sex ('Any Time, Any Place'); we have gender assertion ('This Time', 'You Want This') and we have agenda assertion ('New Agenda', a tough-tender tribute to African-American woman's pride); we have fun ('Funky Big Band'), joy ('Because Of Love') and heartache ('Again'). We also have a *janet. Remixed* album, and a bumper 'Best Of' collection titled *Design Of A Decade 1986/1996,* 17 tracks plus two new ones, 'Runaway' and 'Twenty Foreplay'. Very saucy.

Oh yes, and speaking of *janet.* – the sleeve, those advertisements, those hands. La Janet is posed naked from the hips up, jeans unzipped to just-about-decent level, hands (hers) on head while other hands cup her breasts. How this must have infuriated La Toya Jackson (b La Toya Yvonne, 29 May, 1956), the sister who a few years previously had scandalised the family by posing nude for *Playboy* magazine. Of course, La Toya also married a man many years her senior (Jack Gordon on 5 September, 1989) though age differentials range between 18 and 22 years depending on who is owning up to which particular birthdate at any given time. (Hey! La-Tee might shout in protest, Janet married James De Barge, and that unhappy union was annulled after a beastly 14 months, James' drug problems proving an

unsteady basis for prolonged matrimony.) La Toya also said uncomplimentary things about her family and was generally unhelpful to the cause of maintaining the veneer of America's happy, well-adjusted and most loving family. She also cast doubt on Michael's innocence of charges of child molestation. That girl, her momma said, will do anything for money and publicity. Where could La Toya have got that idea from?

Whatever, La Toya's recordings do nothing to dispel the thought that without the family connection she would not have made so much as a demo. It is ludicrous to assume that everyone in one family can do the same thing well but this family seems to believe that is the case. It is a grossly unfair assumption and places enormous burdens on those members of the family whose talent is not for singing and/or dancing. To be blunt, her voice lacks power, range and character.

She started performing with the brothers' act at the MGM Grand Hotel in Las Vegas in 1972. Eight years later came the first album, *La Toya Jackson* (Polydor, 1981), with disco tracks 'Night Time Lover' (co-written with Michael and produced by him) and 'If You Feel The Funk' getting dance floor action; 'Are You Ready', which was written by Billy Ocean with Ken Gold; La Toya and Janet came up with 'Lovely Is She' and Ollie E Brown, drummer from Stevie Wonder's Wonderlove, produced five of the 10 tracks. A tribe of session players guested from Stevie Wonder and Ray Parker through Patrice Rushen to the Tower of Power and Earth, Wind & Fire horn sections. Bassist Nathan Watts was the star of 'My Love Has Passed You By', which took some doing as Stevie Wonder (harmonica) and Don Myrick (soprano sax) both guested. A second Polydor album, *My Special Love* (1982), was less blessed though it had a dance hit in 'Shake Your Rump To The Funk'.

She left Polydor for Private I and the label début *Heart Don't Lie* (1984) enjoyed considerable publicity because, of course, it was *Thriller* time and everybody wanted to know about brother Michael. At this time, she was in his corner and a year later was the only other Jackson to join Michael in the all-star line-up who recorded 'We Are The World', America's answer to 'Do They Know It's Christmas?', Bob Geldof's Band Aid recording. *Heart* was produced by Amir Bayyan except for 'Frustration', which was co-produced by Howard Hewett, late of Shalamar, and brother Tito. She co-wrote four of the eight tracks, including the title track and 'Hot Potato', a small hit, and managed a risible cover of Prince's 'Private Joy'. Two years later, *Imagination* (Private I, 1986) revealed a more chiselled nose and six out of eight productions by Mike Piccirillo and Gary Goetzman. (The pair had written for George Tobin's productions on Smokey Robinson at the beginning of the Eighties.) Here, however, La Toya's fundamentally limited larynx, which at best is "cute", was a profound stumbling block. Compilations of dubious provenance exist – like *He's My Brother* in Charly's Classic Soul (are they joking?) series – and there was a set in 1988 aptly titled *You Blew It,* with productions by UK pop writers Stock-Aitken-Waterman and US tough team Full Force.

Eldest child Rebbie (that's Ree-bee) Jackson (b Maureen Reilette, 29 May, 1950) clambered on board the sagging bandwagon in 1984, coincidentally enough when the post-*Thriller* feeding frenzy surrounding all things Jackson was at its highest, though one is sure this had little to do with CBS's offer of a recording contract. She'd married at the age of 18, before 'I Want You Back', and set up home well away from the family so if any Jackson had a grasp of "normal" life, she did. Rebbie had done cabaret and session singing but *Centipede* (CBS, 1984) was her first album. The title track, written, produced and arranged by Michael, is the best track but Tito and Randy co-produce with Crusader Wayne Henderson on 'Come Alive It's Saturday Night', written by Jacksons Tito, Jackie, Marlon and Randy (a 'Victory' out-take?) Henderson produced the rest. He met Rebbie through mutual chum Larry Graham, former bassist of Sly & The Family

La Toya Jackson

Stone, leader of Graham Central Station and solo hit-maker thereafter, and in the circs did an acceptable job. She also covered a Prince tune, 'I Feel For You', which Chaka Khan had in the charts at the time, 'A Fork In The Road', a Miracles song from 1965, and 'Play Me (I'm A Jukebox)', co-written by Pam Tillis, daughter of country singer Mel. Her second album, *Reaction* (CBS, 1986), had four producers – Dave Conley, Howie Rice, Reggie Lucas and Tito Jackson/Vassal Benford – nine tracks, a duet with Isaac Hayes on 'Tonight I'm Yours' but none of the material sprang to life. In 1995, she sang a version of Bob Dylan's 'Forever Young' for the *Free Willy 2* movie soundtrack album.

The simple lesson to be drawn from the careers of the Jackson sisters is that finding the right producer is paramount. Ten years younger than La Toya, 16 less than Rebbie, Janet found hers. La Toya has not found a producer who can make the most of an extremely limited singing voice.
After *Centipede,* Rebbie needed to be taken out of the dance market for she was no disco-diva. She still seeks the producer to do that.

KING OF POP
MICHAEL
JACKSON